Haydn R
Junior Er

Ginn and Company Ltd

Acknowledgements

Grateful acknowledgement is made to the following for
permission to use copyright material:

Designed by Michael Soderberg

Illustrated by Barry Rowe, Martin White
Beverly Curl, David Atkinson and Caroline Bilson

© Haydn Richards 1965
Revised edition 1981
Seventeenth impression 1992   089210
ISBN 0 602 22547 7 (without answers)
ISBN 0 602 22619 8 (with answers)
Published by Ginn and Company Ltd
Prebendal House, Parson's Fee,
Aylesbury, Bucks HP20 2QZ
Filmset by Filmtype Services Limited, Scarborough
Printed in Great Britain at the University Press, Cambridge

Preface

The main aim of Haydn Richards Junior English is to enable the pupil to work alone, as far as is possible. For this reason complete lists of the words needed to answer the various exercises are given. Being thus provided with the necessary tools, the pupil should experience little difficulty in doing the work.

The course provides ample and varied practice in all the English topics usually taught in the Junior School. Such simple grammatical terms as are essential to the understanding of the language are introduced at appropriate stages, together with simple definitions, lucid explanations and easy examples.

The meaning of every proverb and idiom dealt with is given, so that these may be used correctly in both writing and conversation.

A noteworthy feature of each book in the series is the detailed alphabetical Contents, facilitating reference to any particular topic by the teacher and the older pupils.

In addition to teaching and testing such topics as Parts of Speech, Opposites, Synonyms, Homophones, Punctuation, Direct and Indirect Speech, Sentence Linkage and Structure, etc., the course includes verbal intelligence exercises designed to stimulate clear thinking, so that by the end of the fourth year the pupil who has worked steadily through the course is well equipped for any entrance examination.

H.R.

Contents

Nouns

The **butcher** gave the **dog** a big meaty **bone**.

butcher is the name of a **person**.
dog is the name of an **animal**.
bone is the name of a **thing**.

A noun is the name of a person, animal or thing.

A   Make a list of the nouns shown in this picture.

B   Find the nouns in these sentences and write them down.

1   The car skidded on the ice and hit a tree.

2   Diamonds, rubies and emeralds are precious stones.

3   There are eleven players in a soccer team.

4   A dog is sometimes called 'man's best friend'.

5   The chief city of a country is called the capital.

6   The heart pumps blood to the body.

7   Rust is caused by oxygen in the air.

8   The referee ordered the offending player off the field.

C   Complete the nouns with missing letters.

1   A r _ _ _ _ _ _ _ _ is a place where you can buy and eat a meal.

2   A h _ _ _ _ _ _ _ _ is a kind of plane capable of rising straight up from the ground and hovering in the air.

3   An artist mixes his colours on a p _ _ _ _ _ _ .

4   A tr _ _ _ _ _ _ has three sides and three angles.

5   A d _ _ _ _ _ is a coin or banknote used in the United States of America and other countries.

1

Verbs

Mother **swept** the floor and **polished** it.

The words **swept** and **polished** are doing words or verbs.

A verb is a word which shows action.

ACORN ST

apologize
bewilder
comprehend
confess
confide
demolish
devour
discuss
expose
extinguish
fortify
glare
hibernate
inhale
loathe
meditate
pester
relax
strive
unite

A Make a list of the verbs in these sentences.

1 Fish breathe through their gills.

2 Many animals hibernate during the winter.

3 Some of them wake and search for food on mild days.

4 After digging the garden, Father raked it well.

5 Brazil produces and exports vast quantities of coffee.

6 The ship struck an iceberg and sank.

B Copy the verbs in the column on the left, then opposite each write the meaning from the list below which matches it.

1 to breathe in
2 to eat like an animal
3 to become less stiff or firm
4 to tell as a secret
5 to spend the winter asleep
6 to uncover; to lay open
7 to express regret
8 to put out; to wipe out
9 to work hard or try hard
10 to understand
11 to make strong
12 to pull or tear down
13 to annoy; to irritate
14 to stare in anger
15 to confuse completely
16 to think quietly
17 to own up to a sin
18 to join together
19 to talk over
20 to regard with disgust

Adjectives

The captain had a **black bushy** beard.

The words **black** and **bushy** describe the captain's beard.

A word which describes a noun is called an adjective.

A   Make a list of the adjectives in these sentences.

1   Rabbits become tame and affectionate when kept as pets.

2   Fruit for jam-making must be sound, ripe, dry and clean.

3   The Canadian prairies are vast plains where huge quantities of wheat are grown.

4   Tame mice are sociable but quarrelsome creatures.

5   The otter has short legs, webbed toes and thick fur.

6   To withstand rough winds, lighthouses are built of interlocking blocks of masonry.

B   Copy the adjectives in the column on the left. Opposite each write the meaning from the list below which matches it.

arrogant	1 richly coloured; splendid
boisterous	2 giving a warm welcome
contemptuous	3 very scornful
distinguished	4 requiring much work
elaborate	5 boastfully proud
frantic	6 successful; thriving
gorgeous	7 well-known; famous
hospitable	8 heavy and clumsy
intelligent	9 bright; shining
laborious	10 quick at learning
memorable	11 self-important
obstinate	12 not moving
pompous	13 very noisy and disorderly
ponderous	14 worked out with great care
prosperous	15 not running or flowing
radiant	16 stubborn
repulsive	17 rough; violent
stagnant	18 causing strong dislike
stationary	19 not to be forgotten
tumultuous	20 wild with rage or pain

Adverbs

1 The troops fought **gallantly**.

Gallantly tells **how** the troops fought. (*manner*)

2 We looked **everywhere** for the lost ball.

Everywhere tells **where** we looked. (*place*)

3 We looked for the lost ball **yesterday**.

Yesterday tells **when** we looked. (*time*)

A word which describes how, where or when an action is performed is called an adverb.

A Make a list of the adverbs in these sentences. After each write **how**, **where** or **when** as required.

1 Nigel washed the dishes carefully.

2 Diana calls to see us frequently.

3 All the rabbits ran away.

4 The two boys wandered aimlessly round the town.

5 The train will be arriving shortly.

6 Dozens of rooks were cawing noisily.

B Complete each sentence by using a suitable adverb from the column on the left.

awkwardly	1 The thief struggled _____ .
bitterly	2 We waited _____ .
contentedly	3 The robin chirped _____ .
courageously	4 The child wept _____ .
distinctly	5 The old man fell _____ .
frugally	6 The champion fought _____ .
gracefully	7 The miser lives _____ .
hungrily	8 He ate his food _____ .
intimately	9 The cows grazed _____ .
merrily	10 He raised his hat _____ .
mournfully	11 The wind howled _____ .
patiently	12 We all laughed _____ .
politely	13 The girls danced _____ .
soundly	14 The baby slept _____ .
uproariously	15 He speaks _____ .
violently	16 I know him _____ .

4

Nouns number

Singular	Plural
chief	chiefs
chimney	chimneys
deer	deer
diary	diaries
Eskimo	Eskimos
factory	factories
goose	geese
hero	heroes
man	men
mouse	mice
ox	oxen
photo	photos
piano	pianos
potato	potatoes
sheaf	sheaves
shelf	shelves
son-in-law	sons-in-law
thief	thieves
turkey	turkeys
wolf	wolves

A   Write the plurals of these words.

1 piano   6 diary   11 deer
2 sheaf   7 goose   12 Eskimo
3 chimney   8 photo   13 factory
4 hero   9 thief   14 son-in-law
5 mouse   10 chief   15 man

B   Write the missing words.

1 factory   many ____
2 turkey   a flock of ____
3 chief   two ____
4 potato   a sack of ____
5 thief   a gang of ____
6 wolf   a pack of ____
7 piano   four ____
8 deer   a herd of ____
9 ox   a team of ____
10 mouse   three ____

C   Rewrite these sentences, changing the nouns in bold type to the plural number and making any other changes which may be necessary.

1 The **thief** removed the **turkey** from the **shelf**.

2 The **Eskimo** was armed with a long **knife**.

3 The **hero** had his **photo** taken.

4 The **child** looked at the little white **mouse**.

5 The **fox** looked longingly at the **goose**.

Attacked by a crow

Silver was almost at the crest when suddenly, from half-way up, there came a high screaming – the sound a rabbit makes, not to call for help or frighten the enemy, but simply out of terror. Fiver and Pipkin, limping behind the others, and conspicuously undersized and tired, were being attacked by the crow. It had flown low along the ground. Then, pouncing, it had aimed a blow of its great bill at Fiver, who just managed to dodge in time. Now it was leaping and hopping among the grass tussocks, striking at the two rabbits with terrible darts of its head. Crows aim at the eyes and Pipkin, sensing this, had buried his head in a clump of rank grass and was trying to burrow farther in. It was he who was screaming.

Hazel covered the distance down the slope in a few seconds. He had no idea what he was going to do and if the crow had ignored him he would probably have been at a loss. But by dashing he distracted its attention and it turned on him. He swerved past it, stopped and, looking back, saw Bigwig come racing in from the opposite side. The crow turned again, struck at Bigwig and missed. Hazel heard its beak hit a pebble in the grass with a sound like a snail-shell when a thrush beats it on a stone. As Silver followed Bigwig, it recovered itself and faced him squarely. Silver stopped short in fear and the crow seemed to dance before him, its great, black wings flapping in a horrible commotion. It was just about to stab when Bigwig ran straight into it from behind and knocked it sideways . . .

Watership Down   Richard Adams

1   Where was Silver when he heard the screaming?
2   Why was Pipkin screaming in this way?
3   Why had the crow chosen Pipkin and Fiver for attack?
4   With what did the crow aim at Fiver?
5   How did Pipkin attempt to escape the crow's attack?
6   Who ran to Pipkin's aid?
7   In what way did this action assist Pipkin?
8   To what does the writer compare the sound made by the crow's beak on the pebble?
9   Which two creatures stood face to face in this fight?
10 What stopped the crow from stabbing at Silver?

Alphabetical order

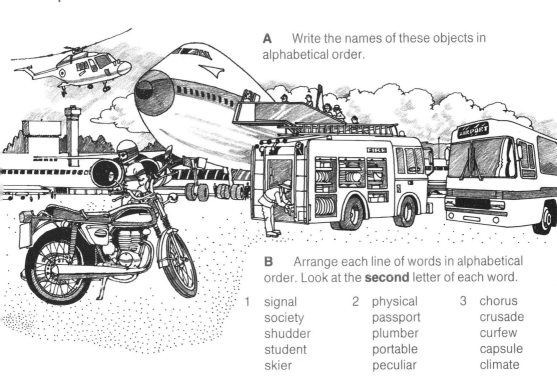

A   Write the names of these objects in alphabetical order.

B   Arrange each line of words in alphabetical order. Look at the **second** letter of each word.

1		2		3	
signal		physical		chorus	
society		passport		crusade	
shudder		plumber		curfew	
student		portable		capsule	
skier		peculiar		climate	

C   Look at the **third** letter of each word when arranging them in alphabetical order.

1		2		3	
blizzard		ground		splint	
blunder		granite		sparrow	
blockade		gruesome		sprawl	
bladder		grease		spectre	
bleak		gristle		spiral	

Look at these words:
hear; **hea**p; **hea**t; **hea**d; **hea**l

Notice that the **first three letters** of each word are the same – **hea**.

To arrange these words in alphabetical order, we must look at the **fourth** letter of each.

These are:
r   p   t   d   l

Letters in alphabetical order:
d   l   p   r   t

Words in alphabetical order:
hea**d**   hea**l**   hea**p**   hea**r**   hea**t**

D   Arrange in alphabetical order, looking at the **fourth** letter.

1		2		3	
catkin		promise		sprout	
cattle		profit		spruce	
catch		produce		sprint	
catalogue		problem		spray	
catgut		proceed		spread	

4		5	
retreat		patriot	
return		patch	
retail		pattern	
retort		patent	
retire		patient	

Verbs past tense and participle

Remember
The Past Tense of a verb does **not** need a helping word.

Example
All the ponds **froze** last night.

The Participle always requires a helping word.

Example
All the ponds **are frozen** this morning.

Helping words
is
are
was
were
has
have
having
had
be
been
being
am

Present tense	Past tense	Past participle
bear	bore	borne
beat	beat	beaten
begin	began	begun
blow	blew	blown
break	broke	broken
burst	burst	burst
choose	chose	chosen
deal	dealt	dealt
drive	drove	driven
drown	drowned	drowned
fight	fought	fought
flee	fled	fled
freeze	froze	frozen
go	went	gone
hang (*thing*)	hung	hung
hang (*person*)	hanged	hanged
hurt	hurt	hurt
lay	laid	laid
lie	lay	lain
mistake	mistook	mistaken
show	showed	shown
slay	slew	slain
think	thought	thought
weave	wove	woven
wring	wrung	wrung

A In each sentence below insert the **past tense** of the verb in bold type.

1 Tom and John _____ a gruelling fight. **fight**

2 The defeated army _____ before their pursuers. **flee**

3 The gladiator _____ his opponent with his sword. **slay**

4 On reaching home Veronica _____ the table for tea. **lay**

5 Dad _____ his hand with an electric drill. **hurt**

6 The spider _____ a web in a very short time. **weave**

7 His teacher _____ him for his twin brother. **mistake**

8 Vast floods _____ hundreds of sheep yesterday. **drown**

B Copy each sentence and complete by inserting the **past participle** of the verb in bold type.

1 We rested after our visitors had _____. **go**

2 He had _____ of a good answer to the question. **think**

3 Several passengers were _____ in the collision. **hurt**

4 David was _____ to captain the school team. **choose**

5 This lovely scarf was _____ by hand. **weave**

6 The condemned man was _____ at eight o'clock in the morning. **hang**

7 Margaret did the sum after her teacher had _____ her the right method. **show**

8 The ground was _____ so the match was postponed. **freeze**

C Insert in each space either the **past tense** or the **past participle** of the verb in bold type, as required.

1 The patient _____ the pain without flinching. **bear**

2 The old ship is to be _____ up next month. **break**

3 Many trees were _____ down during the gale. **blow**

4 Work was _____ on the new school yesterday. **begin**

5 The winner _____ the racing car skilfully. **drive**

6 Our team will probably be _____ in the final. **beat**

7 After lunch Grandma _____ down to rest. **lie**

8 Barbara washed the towel and _____ it out. **wring**

9

Sentences and phrases

Look at this group of words.
Mr. Dobbin bought a new sports car yesterday.

Does it make sense? Yes.
Does it contain a verb? Yes.

Then it is a **sentence**.

A sentence is a group of words which make sense. Every sentence contains a verb.

Look at this group of words.
Without even a glance at his book

Does it make sense? No.
Does it contain a verb? No.

Then it is not a sentence; it is a **phrase**.

A   Say whether each group of words is a sentence or a phrase.

1   Most trees shed their leaves every autumn.

2   Early in the autumn of every year

3   The majority of men throughout the entire world

4   Most people work.

5   The farmer chased the boys.

6   Waving his stick and shouting angrily.

7   Dogs with long hair and broad feet

8   Dogs bark.

B   Form a sentence from each phrase below.

1   Whilst waiting for the bus ....

2   The boy who found the purse ....

3   Having finished his homework ....

4   .... and posted it in the letter box.

5   .... because she is very fond of chocolates.

6   .... but the doctor would not allow him to get up.

7   The milkman .... on our doorstep every morning.

8   The goalkeeper .... and tipped it over the bar.

9   A huge fire .... was blazing in the dining-room grate.

10   The hunter raised his rifle .... with one shot.

Nouns gender

Masculine	Feminine
bachelor	spinster
boar	sow
buck	doe
bull	cow
conductor	conductress
drake	duck
emperor	empress
heir	heiress
host	hostess
lord	lady
marquis	marchioness
mayor	mayoress
nephew	niece
peacock	peahen
proprietor	proprietress
ram	ewe
sir	madam
stag	hind
widower	widow
wizard	witch

A   Write the **feminine** gender of:

1	sir	6	emperor
2	bachelor	7	marquis
3	lord	8	bullock
4	mayor	9	nephew
5	peacock	10	heir

B   Write the **masculine** gender of:

1	duck	6	hostess
2	sow	7	niece
3	widow	8	ewe
4	witch	9	doe
5	hind	10	empress

C   In each sentence change the **masculine** noun to the **feminine** gender.

1   The proprietor of the guest house welcomed every guest.

2   A beautiful peacock strutted about the lawn.

3   The conductor rang the bell and the bus started.

4   He sent a handsome present to his nephew.

5   The marquis is cruising in the Mediterranean.

6   The letter began, Dear Sir.

D   Complete each sentence by using a noun of the opposite gender to that in bold type.

1   Farmer Bond keeps ten pigs, two **boars** and eight ____ .

2   The **drake** swam on the pond while the ____ waddled round the farmyard with her little ones.

3   A record price was paid for the ____ and the **cow**.

4   **Lord** and ____ Bryce were at the garden party.

5   The wool on the **ram** was thicker than that on the ____ .

6   The red deer **stag** had antlers; the ____ had none.

Toad and company

When they were quite ready the now triumphant Toad led his companions to the paddock and set them to capture the old grey horse, who, without having been consulted, and to his own extreme annoyance, had been told off by Toad for the dustiest job in this dusty expedition. He frankly preferred the paddock, and took a great deal of catching. Meantime Toad packed the lockers still tighter with necessaries, and hung nose-bags, nets of onions, bundles of hay, and baskets from the bottom of the cart. At last the horse was caught and harnessed, and they set off, all talking at once, each animal either trudging by the side of the cart or sitting on the shaft, as the humour took him. It was a golden afternoon. The smell of the dust they kicked up was rich and satisfying; out of thick orchards on either side of the road birds called and whistled to them cheerily; good-natured wayfarers, passing them, gave them "Good day," or stopped to say nice things about their beautiful cart; and rabbits, sitting at their front doors in the hedgerows, held up their fore-paws and said, "O my! O my! O my!"

    Late in the evening, tired and happy and miles from home, they drew up on a remote common far from habitations, turned the horse loose to graze, and ate their simple supper sitting on the grass by the side of the cart.

The Wind in the Willows   Kenneth Grahame

1   What did Toad set his companions to do?
2   Why did the old grey horse take a good deal of catching?
3   What did Toad hang from the bottom of the cart?
4   What were the animals doing when they were not trudging by the side of the cart?
5   How did the birds in the orchards greet the travellers?
6   What did the wayfarers say when they passed the travellers?
7   What did these people say when they stopped to talk to them?
8   Where did Toad and Company draw up late that evening?
9   What did they do with the horse?
10 Where did they eat their supper?

Nouns formation

Verb	Noun
abolish	abolition
accuse	accusation
acquaint	acquaintance
advertise	advertisement
advise	advice
applaud	applause
choose	choice
complain	complaint
complete	completion
converse	conversation
deceive	deceit
decide	decision
destroy	destruction
explain	explanation
explode	explosion
imagine	imagination
inquire	inquiry
pronounce	pronunciation
pursue	pursuit
satisfy	satisfaction

A   Copy these phrases, inserting in the spaces the nouns formed from the verbs in bold type.

1 a lively _____   **imagine**
2 sound _____   **advise**
3 a violent _____   **explode**
4 widespread _____   **destroy**
5 a long _____   **converse**
6 a full-page _____   **advertise**
7 loud _____   **applaud**
8 correct _____   **pronounce**
9 a false _____   **accuse**
10 a serious _____   **complain**

B   Complete each sentence by inserting the noun formed from the verb in bold type.

1 Purchasers have a _____ of several colours.   **choose**

2 In 1833 an Act was passed for the _____ of slavery in the British Empire.   **abolish**

3 Any _____ to increase pensions will be welcomed.   **decide**

4 He listened patiently to his teacher's _____ .   **explain**

5 The work was done to the customer's _____ .   **satisfy**

6 Several hunters went in _____ of the lion.   **pursue**

7 An _____ is a search for truth, knowledge or information.   **inquire**

8 The work on the new road is nearing _____ .   **complete**

9 _____ means making a person believe to be true something which is false.   **deceive**

10 He is not really a friend, just an _____ .   **acquaint**

Adjectives formation

Some adjectives are formed simply by adding the letter **y** to a noun.

Examples   cloud   cloudy
              mould   mouldy
              marsh   marshy

When the noun ends with **e**, this letter is dropped before the **y** is added.

Examples   shade   shady
              smoke   smoky
              juice   juicy

When **y** is added to some nouns the last letter is doubled.

Examples   sun   sunny
              mud   muddy
              star   starry

A   Use the adjective formed from the noun in bold type to fill each space. Copy the phrases in your book.

1 A material covered with **fluff**   a _____ material
2 A voice with a **squeak**   a _____ voice
3 Foods containing much **starch**   _____ foods
4 A man of great **wealth**   a _____ man
5 A morning with much **frost**   a _____ morning

B   Insert in each space the adjective formed from the noun in bold type. Remember to drop the final **e**.

1 A path with many **stones**   a _____ path
2 Hair in which there is a **wave**   _____ hair
3 Dishes covered with **grease**   _____ dishes
4 A day when a **breeze** is blowing   a _____ day
5 A dinner with a nice **taste**   a _____ dinner
6 A beach covered with **pebbles**   a _____ beach

C   Form the adjective from the noun in bold type to fill each space. Remember to double the final letter.

1 An animal covered with **fur**   a _____ animal
2 A sound like that of **tin**   a _____ sound
3 Wood full of **knots**   _____ wood
4 Land which is largely **bog**   _____ land
5 A speech containing much **wit**   a _____ speech
6 A hand which is more **skin** than flesh   a _____ hand

Direct speech

When we write the words spoken by someone we put **speech marks** round them. These are also called **inverted commas**.

Examples

"Please shut the door after you," said Rodney irritably.

The farmer shouted angrily, "Get out of that hayfield."

"If you don't work hard," said the teacher, "you will never succeed."

Notice how **"** is used at the beginning of the words spoken and **"** at the end.

A   Copy these sentences and put speech marks round the words actually spoken.

1   Your shoelace is undone, Barbara, said Wendy.

2   Did you remember to bring a loaf, Sonia? asked her mother.

3   These cauliflowers were cut this morning, madam, said the greengrocer.

4   Keep him in bed for a few days, advised the doctor.

B   Copy these sentences, putting speech marks where required.

1   The dentist said, you should have that tooth filled.

2   Linda remarked, this is the tastiest meal I have had for a long time.

3   Handing him ten pence the old lady said, thank you for your help, my boy.

4   The auctioneer asked, is there any advance on fifty pounds?

C   Copy these sentences and put speech marks round the words actually spoken.

1   Please sir, said Oliver Twist to the master I want some more.

2   Oh, dear, sighed the old lady, I have lost the key of the house.

3   You will have to hurry, Mary, exclaimed her mother, or you will be late for school.

4   Stand to attention, shouted the sergeant, and hold your heads up.

Other words for said and asked

Using **said** or **asked** too often makes a composition monotonous.

Choose the most suitable word from the list on the left to complete each sentence.

A

admitted
announced
boasted
remarked
shouted
stammered
urged
whispered

1 "It is much colder today than it was yesterday," ____ the old boatman.

2 "Hush, Pamela," ____ her mother, "or you will wake the baby."

3 "Go on, Tony," ____ his teacher, "try to beat David's jump."

4 "All hands on deck," ____ the skipper of the trawler.

5 "I b-b-beg your pardon," ____ the frightened boy.

6 "Yes, it was I who broke the basin," ____ Carol.

7 "I am easily the best reader in the class," ____ Alan.

8 "The school will be closed all next week," ____ the headmaster.

B

coaxed
complained
grumbled
inquired
ordered
prophesied
protested
replied

1 "Prepare the theatre for an emergency operation at once," ____ the surgeon.

2 "Is this the way to the Post Office, please?" ____ the stranger.

3 "Yes," ____ the policeman, "keep straight on for about fifty metres and you will see it on your left."

4 "Please, Mummy, may I have just one more chocolate?" ____ Elizabeth.

5 "Your prices are far too high," ____ the customer to the grocer.

6 "I think we are going to have a very warm summer this year," ____ Aunt Jane.

7 "Your dog has been worrying my sheep, Mr. Bath," ____ the farmer.

8 "I get all the tedious jobs," ____ the shop assistant.

Collective nouns

actors	company
angels	host
arrows	sheaf; quiver
bells	peal
chicks	brood
directors	board
eggs	clutch
lions	pride
locusts	plague; swarm
magistrates	bench
minstrels	troupe
pilgrims	band
thieves	gang
singers	choir
spectators	crowd
stars	cluster
swallows	flight
teachers	staff
trees	clump
worshippers	congregation

Write the missing words.

A

1 a ____ of singers
2 a ____ of teachers
3 a ____ of chicks
4 a ____ of bells
5 a ____ of actors
6 a ____ of locusts
7 a ____ of spectators
8 a ____ of thieves
9 a ____ of lions
10 a ____ of swallows

B

1 a host of ____
2 a clump of ____
3 a cluster of ____
4 a band of ____
5 a board of ____
6 a troupe of ____
7 a quiver of ____
8 a bench of ____
9 a congregation of ____
10 a clutch of ____

C Write the collective nouns needed to complete these sentences.

1 The ____ of pilgrims halted before the mosque.

2 A ____ of locusts devoured every growing plant.

3 The mother hen was accompanied by her ____ of chicks.

4 Under a small ____ of trees a tent had been pitched.

5 Several plays have been performed by this brilliant ____ of actors.

6 The police are searching for a ____ of car thieves.

7 The ____ of directors met to consider their company's losses.

8 The match was watched by a huge ____ of spectators.

9 In his dream Jacob saw a ____ of angels.

10 The children saw a ____ of swallows making for the sea.

Wildlife in danger

It is a disturbing fact that today many different kinds of wild animal throughout the world are in danger of extinction. The reasons for this are many and varied, but we must largely blame pollution, pesticides, the disturbance of the animals' natural environment and man's greed and thoughtlessness.

Industry has grown enormously, and it has become common practice for factories to dispose of waste matter in streams and rivers, causing great loss of river life. Modern agricultural methods include the use of pesticides which effectively control insects classified as pests, but which also destroy many that are not. An increase in population has meant more building – and with it the destruction of much of the countryside that provides habitat for wild animals. To satisfy man's selfish desires the polar bear in North America is under threat, hunted by sportsmen; in Borneo and Sumatra the orang-utan has become part of a smuggling racket; in South America the chinchilla is almost extinct because its fur is in demand; whales are massacred world-wide for the oil and food they yield. These are only a few of the species under threat.

But the problem is receiving world-wide recognition, and some action is being taken. To name a few examples – sewage pollution in the River Thames has been greatly reduced; a ban on trading in some furs has been agreed; and organisations like Friends of the Earth do valuable work in this deserving cause.

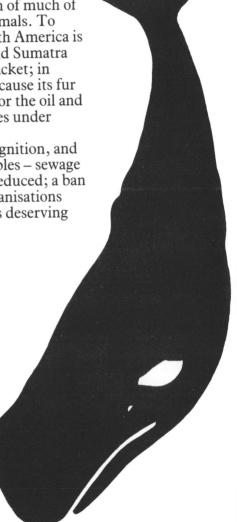

1   Give in your own words two reasons why some species of wild animal may become extinct.
2   Why has it become common practice for factories to pollute streams and rivers?
3   Which insects are intended to be destroyed by pesticides?
4   What has brought about the destruction of much of the countryside?
5   Why is the polar bear in North America under threat?
6   Which countries have problems with smuggling?
7   Which animal is hunted for its fur?
8   Why are whales hunted in such large numbers?
9   What is being done to help preserve our river life?
10 Name one other way in which wild life is currently helped.

Fun with words

a _ _ _ _   a male farm animal

b _ _ _ _ _ _   a missile fired from
a rifle

Word (**a**) is bull

Word (**b**) is bullet

Now try the exercise below. Remember that each dash stands for a letter, and that the second word of each pair is formed by adding letters to the first word.

A

1   **a** _ _ _ _   a large stringed instrument
     b _ _ _ _ _ _ _   a spear used in hunting whales

2   **a** _ _ _ _   a man who lives in a monastery
     b _ _ _ _ _ _   an agile and mischievous animal

3   **a** _ _ _   a young goat
     b _ _ _ _ _ _   to steal a person by force

4   **a** _ _ _   an article of headgear
     b _ _ _ _ _ _ _   a small axe

5   **a** _ _ _ _   an American coin of small value
     b _ _ _ _ _ _   the middle

6   **a** _ _ _ _   a place where ships can shelter
     b _ _ _ _ _ _ _   a part or a share

7   **a** _ _ _ _   stop
     b _ _ _ _ _ _   a rope or strap for leading an animal

8   **a** _ _ _ _   a man who entertains guests
     b _ _ _ _ _ _ _   of an enemy; unfriendly

9   **a** _ _ _   a male child
     b _ _ _ _ _ _ _   to refuse to have anything to do with

10   **a** _ _ _ _   a lump; a large quantity together
      b _ _ _ _ _ _ _ _   wholesale; pitiless slaughter

B

In a certain code
the figures   **5 2 9 7 4 6 3 1 8**
stand for the word   C O M P A N I E S

Write the words for:
1   **8 5 4 9 7**
2   **5 2 9 1 8**
3   **7 4 6 3 5**
4   **8 6 3 7 1**
5   **8 7 4 5 1**

Write the figures for:
6   C A P E S
7   O P E N S
8   S P I C E
9   P I A N O
10   S C O N E

Using the right adjective

A Copy the adjectives in column **a** in your exercise book in the order given. Opposite each write the noun in column **b** which matches it.

a	b
frantic	slope
antique	allowance
affectionate	drugs
formidable	grip
palatable	clothes
injurious	daughter
threadbare	struggles
meagre	task
precipitous	furniture
relentless	meal

B Choose the word from the list on the left which will complete each sentence correctly.

shrewd
vivid
candid
riotous
abundant
luscious
secluded
righteous
sumptuous
prosperous

1 The traveller had many ＿＿ memories of his jungle adventures.

2 The peach is a ＿＿ fruit.

3 Sir Walter is the managing director of a ＿＿ business.

4 The ＿＿ businessman made a profit.

5 A ＿＿ feast was held in the emperor's honour.

6 The boys were rocking with ＿＿ laughter.

7 The town is proud of its ＿＿ supply of water.

8 He gave them his ＿＿ opinion of their actions.

9 At the bottom of the garden was a ＿＿ nook with an oak seat beneath a shady tree.

10 The insult filled the woman with ＿＿ indignation.

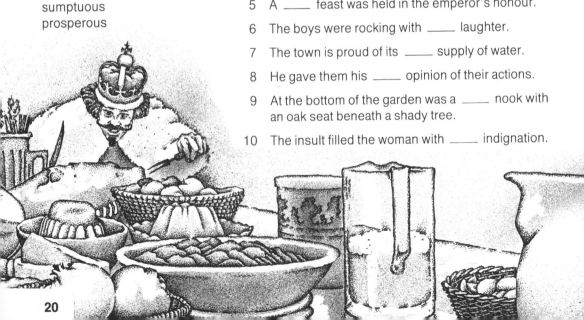

Pronouns

a John told Susan that John would lend Susan a book.

b John told Susan that **he** would lend **her** a book.

Instead of repeating the word **John**, the word **he** is used in (**b**).

Instead of repeating the word **Susan**, the word **her** is used.

A word which is used instead of a noun is called a pronoun.

herself

her
it

itself

A Rewrite these sentences, using pronouns from the list on the left in place of the words in bold type.

he
it
we
us
she
her
his
him
them
they

1 Anne told Jennifer that **Anne** would knit a cardigan for **Jennifer**.

2 When Colin was given a dog **Colin** trained **the dog** to beg.

3 Brian and I are good friends. **Brian and I** go everywhere together.

4 As Roger and I approached the farmyard gate a big dog barked at **Roger and me**.

5 The teacher sent for Robin and Alan. The teacher told **Robin and Alan** to stay in after school.

6 The two girls knew that **the two girls** would be late.

7 Andrew was sad because the stolen bicycle was **Andrew's**.

B Insert one of the pronouns in the list on the left in each sentence.

myself
itself
yourself
ourselves
yourselves
herself

1 You boys must make _____ useful in the garden.

2 Did you make this table _____ , Spencer?

3 The hedgehog can roll _____ into a prickly ball.

4 I can work the sum by _____ , thank you.

5 Janet certainly thinks _____ somebody of importance.

6 We built the house _____ .

Homophones

Some words are pronounced like other words but are different in spelling and meaning,
e.g. main, mane
  bear, bare.

Such words are called homophones.

air	what we breathe
heir	one entitled to a dead person's property
allowed	permitted
aloud	loud enough to be heard
beach	the sea-shore
beech	a tree
boy	a male child
buoy	a floating marker for ships
brake	a device to check speed
break	to cause something to come into pieces
cereal	wheat, barley and oats are all cereals
serial	a story or film appearing in parts
check	to stop; a squared pattern
cheque	an order to a bank to pay money
coarse	rough
course	a track; an onward movement
currant	a dried grape
current	a flow of water, air, etc.
foul	filthy; wicked; vile
fowl	a bird

A Choose the correct word from the pair above to complete each sentence.

1 **cereal   serial**
Cornflakes are his favourite ____.

2 **currant   current**
These ____ buns are delicious.

3 **foul   fowl**
Fulham were awarded a free-kick for a ____ on their goalkeeper.

4 **air   heir**
Prince Charles is ____ to the throne.

5 **break   brake**
New blocks had to be fitted to the front ____ of the bicycle.

B Write five pairs of words to complete these sentences.

1 Father paid by ____ for his new ____ suit.

2 The ____ who fell overboard swam to a nearby ____ .

3 Talking ____ is not ____ in the reading room of the library.

4 Racing was difficult because the grass on the ____ was long and ____ .

5 Not far from the sandy ____ grew a clump of ____ trees.

Abbreviations

Abbreviations are shortened forms of words or phrases.

Learn this list, then do the exercises.

A.A.	Automobile Association
c/o	care of
Dept.	Department
H.R.H.	His (Her) Royal Highness
J.P.	Justice of the Peace
Ltd.	Limited
M.D.	Doctor of Medicine
M.P.	Member of Parliament
M.O.H.	Medical Officer of Health
N.S.P.C.C.	National Society for the Prevention of Cruelty to Children
O.H.M.S.	On Her Majesty's Service
p.c.	postcard
R.N.	Royal Navy
R.S.P.C.A.	Royal Society for the Prevention of Cruelty to Animals
U.N.	United Nations
Tel.	Telephone; Telegraph

A   Write the meanings of the abbreviations in bold type.

1   The widow wrote to her **M.P.** about her compensation.

2   The letter was addressed to the Sales **Dept**.

3   An inspector of the **N.S.P.C.C.** called to inspect the house.

4   Tim's holiday address is **c/o** Mrs. Baines, 15 High St., Burland.

5   A large crowd gathered to greet **H.R.H.** Princess Margaret.

6   The matter has been reported to the **R.S.P.C.A.**

7   I will send you a **p.c.** as soon as I arrive.

8   The warrant for the arrest of the culprit was signed by a **J.P.**

B   Give the meaning of each abbreviation in bold type.

1   On the notepaper was printed: **Tel.** Bury 2385.

2   No postage is payable on letters and parcels sent **O.H.M.S.**

3   The building of the **R.N.** Barracks at Devonport was begun in 1879.

4   The **A.A.** was founded in London in 1905.

5   Both Britain and America are members of the **U.N.**

6   A lecture on the evils of smoking was given by Charles Rennie, **M.D.**

7   The **M.O.H.** told people to boil all drinking water.

Rikki-tikki and Darzee

Then Rikki-tikki went out into the garden to see what was to be seen. It was a large garden, only half-cultivated, with bushes as big as summer-houses of Marshal Niel roses, lime and orange trees, clumps of bamboo, and thickets of high grass. Rikki-tikki licked his lips. "This is a splendid hunting-ground," he said, and his tail grew bottle-brushy at the thought of it, and he scuttled up and down the garden, snuffing here and there till he heard very sorrowful voices in a thornbush.

It was Darzee, the tailor-bird, and his wife. They had made a beautiful nest by pulling two big leaves together and stitching them up the edges with fibres, and had filled the hollow with cotton and downy fluff. The nest swayed to and fro, as they sat on the rim and cried.

"What is the matter?" asked Rikki-tikki.

"We are very miserable," said Darzee. "One of our babies fell out of the nest yesterday, and Nag ate him."

"H'm!" said Rikki-tikki, "that is very sad – but I am a stranger here. Who is Nag?"

Darzee and his wife only cowered down in the nest without answering, for from the thick grass at the foot of the bush there came a low hiss – a horrid cold sound that made Rikki-tikki jump back two clear feet. Then inch by inch out of the grass rose up the head and spread hood of Nag, the big black cobra, and he was five feet long from tongue to tail.

The Jungle Book   Rudyard Kipling.

1   Why did Rikki-tikki lick his lips?
2   What change came over Rikki-tikki's tail as he thought about this?
3   What did Rikki-tikki hear as he scuttled up and down the garden?
4   How do tailor-birds make a nest?
5   Why were Darzee and his wife crying?
6   Where did the low hiss come from?
7   What did Darzee and his wife do when they heard this noise?
8   What effect did this sound have on Rikki-tikki?
9   How long was Nag from tongue to tail?

Letter writing

Alastair Brooks saw this advertisement in a magazine.

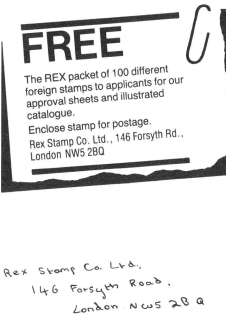

FREE

The REX packet of 100 different foreign stamps to applicants for our approval sheets and illustrated catalogue.
Enclose stamp for postage.
Rex Stamp Co. Ltd., 146 Forsyth Rd., London NW5 2BQ

19 Jubilee Road,
Granton,
Kent GN7 4CP

Rex Stamp Co. Ltd.,
146 Forsyth Road,
London NW5

Dear Sirs,
Please send me the Rex free packet of foreign stamps, also a selection of approval sheets and a copy of your illustrated catalogue.
I enclose stamps for postage.
Yours faithfully,
Alastair Brooks.

Rex Stamp Co. Ltd.,
146 Forsyth Road,
London NW5 2BQ

This is how he addressed the envelope.

This is the letter he wrote.

Points to remember:

a   Keep to the form of letter shown, giving your full address.

b   State exactly what you require, making your letter as brief as possible.

c   If requested to enclose stamps or a postal order, make sure you do so.

d   Address the envelope plainly and fully, and see that it bears a stamp for the correct postage.

1   Write a letter to the Planet Novelty Co. Ltd., 49 Greenham Avenue, London E12 SA16 for a copy of their price-list of conjuring tricks, enclosing stamps for postage.

2   The Medico Co. Ltd., Grove Buildings, Anson Street, Birmingham B12 4EH, offer a free sample tube of Atlas toothpaste to all applicants enclosing stamps for postage. Send for a sample.

3   Write to the Mekko Model Co. Ltd., 37 Bilton Road, London SE16 8RL for a copy of their illustrated catalogue of model railways, aircraft, racing cars and boats, which will be sent post free.

Occupations

A Write the names of these occupations.

announcer   plumber
postwoman   butcher
chef   chemist
florist   waitress
nurse   steeplejack
jeweller   tobacconist
librarian   undertaker
cricketer   upholsterer

B Select the word from the list on the left which will complete each sentence.

1 The _____ at the public library has three excellent assistants.

2 The _____ at the corner sells lots of different sweets and chocolates.

3 The _____ at the beach café served us with tea very quickly.

4 The _____ had a large selection of medicines and pills.

5 The _____ offered Maisie a gold watch at a reduced price.

6 The twins went to the _____ to buy their mother a bouquet of flowers.

7 The _____ displays all his meats on trays in his shop window.

8 The _____ climbed to the top of the church steeple to inspect the damage done by the gale.

9 Our _____ uses her bicycle on her rounds.

10 The _____ took Tom's temperature and pulse every four hours.

Group names

A Give the name of the group to which these objects belong.

B Choose the word in the column on the left which belongs to each of the groups below. Give the name of each group.

baker
silver
alligator
synagogue
villa
venison

Example   1 **venison**   names of meats

1	beef	2	cathedral	3	cobra
	pork		temple		crocodile
	lamb		church		adder
	mutton		chapel		lizard

4	house	5	copper	6	grocer
	bungalow		gold		butcher
	mansion		iron		fruiterer
	cottage		lead		fishmonger

C Draw four columns and write the headings:

Weapons   Vessels   Furniture   Footwear

Then place the words below in their correct groups. There will be six words in each group.

liner	sandals	spear	wardrobe
clogs	submarine	boots	pistol
cupboard	dagger	sideboard	cruiser
rifle	armchair	yacht	cabinet
trawler	shoes	sword	wellingtons
table	schooner	slippers	revolver

Comparing adjectives

There are **three** degrees of adjectives.

1 The **positive degree**.
   Used for one person or thing e.g. tall

2 The **comparative degree**.
   Used in comparing two persons or things e.g. taller

3 The **superlative degree**.
   Used in comparing more than two persons or things e.g. tallest

We can add **-er** and **-est** to many adjectives without any change in spelling, e.g. strong, stronger, strongest.

But look out for these spelling changes.

a Dropping final **e**.
   e.g. wide, wider, widest

b Changing **y** to **i**.
   e.g. happy, happier, happiest

c Doubling the last letter.
   e.g. hot, hotter, hottest.

When comparing longer adjectives the words **more** and **most**, or **less** and **least** are placed before them.

Example
Jill is the **most reliable** person for the job.

Roger is **fat**.   Rex is **fatter**.

A   Copy and complete this table.

	Positive degree	Comparative degree	Superlative degree
1	lovely	——	——
2	large	——	——
3	hot	——	——
4	noisy	——	——
5	slim	——	——
6	wise	——	——
7	wet	——	——
8	wealthy	——	——
9	fine	——	——
10	greedy	——	——

B   Complete each sentence, using the **comparative degree** or the **superlative degree** of the adjective in bold type.

1 Robinson is the ____ workman of the two.   **capable**

2 She is easily the ____ girl of the whole school.   **intelligent**

3 Julian is the ____ of the two brothers.   **generous**

Angus is the **fattest**.

Some adjectives cannot be compared in the ways shown; they are irregular.

4 Jean chose the ____ dress in the shop. **expensive**

5 A miner's work is ____ than a farmer's. **dangerous**

6 Many people consider the Taj Mahal to be the ____ building in the world. **wonderful**

7 The manager has the ____ job in the works. **important**

8 This is the ____ book of the two. **interesting**

Positive degree	Comparative degree	Superlative degree
good	better	best
bad	worse	worst
ill	worse	worst
many	more	most
much	more	most
little	less	least

C   Write the correct degree of the adjective which will complete each sentence.

1 This is the ____ blizzard I have ever seen. **bad**

2 The patient was very ill yesterday but he is even ____ today. **ill**

3 Both boys read well, but David is the ____ reader. **good**

4 Your cold is ____ than mine. **bad**

5 Dorothy is the ____ singer in the school choir. **good**

6 August is the month when guest-houses have the ____ bookings. **many**

7 £1 is the ____ amount that can be invested. **small**

8 Geoffrey has little common sense; Francis has even ____ . **little**

The score card

Below you will find the first innings score card of the Kenville Cricket Club in their annual match against Royford Cricket Club. Look at the questions which follow, study the score card, and then write your answers.

Kenville – First innings

R. Dale; b Gibson	41
J. W. Gray; c Jagger, b Barlow	52
B. R. Lock; lbw Rank	27
W. Smith; c Jagger, b Rank	9
A. Booth; c Robinson, b Moss	83
T. E. Dexter; not out	35
C. Green; c and b Gibson	6
E. F. Clark; st Jagger, b Moss	1
L. Jones; c Thomson, b Moss	0
D. Macmillan; b Moss	0
S. Taylor; st Jagger, b Rank	3
Extras	8
Total	

1   Who was the highest scorer?

2   How many short of a century was his score?

3   How many batsmen were clean bowled? Who were they?

4   Who was bowled for a "duck"?

5   Which bowler made a catch off his own bowling?

6   Which of the batsmen was undefeated at the end of the innings?

7   Who was caught before he had scored?

8   Who was out leg before wicket?

9   What was the name of Royford's wicket-keeper?

10   Do you think he played well or not? Give reasons for your answer.

11   One of the four bowlers performed the "hat trick". Who do you think this was?

12   How many runs will Royford have to make for a first innings lead?

Conjunctions

Paul closed his book.
He put it away.   *two sentences*

Paul closed his book **and** put
it away.   *one sentence*

The word **and** joins the two
sentences.

**A word which joins two groups
of words or two sentences
is called a conjunction.**

so
as
but
for
and
since
while
because

if
or
after
until
where
unless
although
whether

A   Join each pair of sentences below, using a
suitable conjunction from the list on the left.

1 The boy got out of bed.
   He stretched his arms.

2 We intended to swim.
   The weather was too cold.

3 The cinema was full.
   We went back home.

4 The children made their way home.
   It was getting dark.

5 Ben made some tea.
   His mother bathed the baby.

6 The wind was icy cold.
   It was still winter.

7 She was very unpopular.
   She was so sarcastic.

8 You can do it yourself.
   You are so clever.

B   Insert a suitable conjunction in each space.

1 Would you like a cup of tea ____ would you prefer
   coffee?

2 There will be more accidents at the crossroads
   ____ a roundabout is built there soon.

3 The plan was abandoned ____ much money had
   been spent on it.

4 I enjoyed the film ____ I had seen it before.

5 We intend to go ____ it rains or not.

6 Your arithmetic will improve ____ you always check
   your working.

7 Please do nothing ____ you hear from me.

8 The pupils visited St. Paul's Cathedral ____ they
   were shown the Whispering Gallery.

Opposites using a prefix

The opposites of some words can be formed by writing before them **un**, **in**, **il**, **dis**, **ir** or **im**.

un
aware
certain
favourable
fortunate
grateful
important
kind
necessary
popular
usual

dis
appear
approve
connect
continue
courteous
honest
obedient
orderly
regard
similar

in
considerate
efficient
equality
frequent
gratitude
human
sane

ir
regular
responsible
reverent

im
movable
patient
perfect
probable
proper

il
legal

A   Form the opposites of these words, using prefixes.

1   sane
2   aware
3   human
4   usual
5   obedient
6   approve
7   equality
8   similar
9   certain
10   perfect
11   gratitude
12   regard
13   continue
14   considerate
15   orderly

B   Select a word from the list to complete each sentence.

1   An ____ event is one which will probably never happen.

2   An object which cannot be moved is ____ .

3   An ____ person gives no thanks for kindnesses received.

4   Another word for ____ is unlawful.

5   An ____ person is not responsible for his actions.

6   An ____ article is one you can do without.

7   The word ____ means unlucky.

8   A ____ person is rude and ill-mannered.

C   Use these phrases in sentences of your own, but give the word in bold type an opposite meaning.

1   a **popular** man
2   **regular** attendance
3   an **efficient** worker
4   an **important** town
5   **favourable** weather
6   a **proper** remark

People

exile	A person banished from his native country
genius	An exceptionally brainy or gifted person
hypocrite	Pretends to be better than he really is
lunatic	A person who is mad
mimic	Imitates the voice and actions of others
pedestrian	Travels about on foot
prophet	Foretells coming events
traitor	Betrays his country, friends or any trust
tyrant	Uses his power to oppress others
vandal	Wilfully damages or destroys property

PEDESTRIANS ONLY

A   Give one word for each of the following.

1   A person who attends church regularly yet leads an evil life in secret

2   A man who sells his country's secrets to a foreign power

3   A king who treats his subjects harshly

4   A person who is not in his right mind

5   A person who has not seen his native land for many years

B   Complete each sentence by using a word from the list.

1   The event was foretold by a ____ who lived in Israel.

2   A ____ who crossed the road without looking both ways was knocked down by a car.

3   Shakespeare, who wrote some of the world's best plays, was a ____ .

4   A ____ had uprooted shrubs in the park and smashed several windows in the pavilion.

5   The ____ in the variety show gave wonderful imitations of television stars.

Proper adjectives

A **proper adjective** is one formed from a **proper noun**, which is the name of a particular person, place or thing.

Alps	Alpine
Belgium	Belgian
China	Chinese
Cyprus	Cypriot
Denmark	Danish
Finland	Finnish
Greece	Greek
Holland	Dutch
Iceland	Icelandic
Israel	Israeli
Malta	Maltese
Mexico	Mexican
Norway	Norwegian
Poland	Polish
Portugal	Portuguese
Spain	Spanish
Sweden	Swedish
Switzerland	Swiss
Turkey	Turkish
Venice	Venetian

A   Copy these phrases, inserting in each the **proper adjective** formed from the proper noun in bold type.

1   A ____ dance   **Spain**
2   A ____ goddess   **Greece**
3   ____ bacon   **Denmark**
4   A ____ restaurant   **China**
5   ____ bulbs   **Holland**
6   ____ oranges   **Israel**
7   A ____ cross   **Malta**
8   The ____ fiords   **Norway**
9   An ____ village   **Alps**
10   ____ timber   **Sweden**

B   Complete each sentence below by using a **proper adjective** from the list on the left.

1   Many Britons spend their holidays on the ____ coast.   **Belgium**

2   Tampico is a ____ port.   **Mexico**

3   Many ____ refugees have settled down in Britain.   **Poland**

4   ____ watches are renowned for their reliability.   **Switzerland**

5   A fez is a felt cap with a long tassel formerly worn by ____ men.   **Turkey**

6   ____ wines are famous, the best known being Port Wine.   **Portugal**

7   Thousands of fish were landed by the ____ trawlers.   **Iceland**

8   The long narrow boats used on ____ canals are called gondolas.   **Venice**

Nouns possession

A

To make a **singular** noun show possession add **'s**.

Examples

the apron belonging to mother
mother**'s** apron

the beak of the duck
the duck**'s** beak

1. the dress belonging to Ann
2. the sword belonging to the knight
3. the thimble belonging to the tailor
4. the block belonging to the butcher
5. the pads belonging to the cricketer
6. the jaws of the lion
7. the reward of the winner
8. the gloves of the boxer
9. the jokes of the comedian

B

To make a **plural** noun **ending with s** show possession add **'**.

Examples

the football belonging to the boys
the boy**s'** football

the necks of the swans
the swan**s'** necks

1. the lamps belonging to the miners
2. the tusks belonging to the elephants
3. the quarters belonging to the sailors
4. the room belonging to the porters
5. the playground belonging to the girls
6. the tails of the monkeys
7. the wings of the insects
8. the nests of the birds
9. the cloakroom for ladies

C

To make a **plural** noun **which does not end with s** show possession, add **'s** just as with a singular noun.

Examples

the work of the men
the men**'s** work

fashions for women
women**'s** fashions

1. handbags for women
2. the yokes belonging to the oxen
3. the tails belonging to the mice
4. the helmets belonging to the policemen
5. toys for children
6. shoes for men
7. the camp of the airmen
8. the feet of the frogmen
9. the honks of the geese

Sea-lions

Sea-lions bear some resemblance to seals, though they are much larger. When fully grown they are from twelve to twenty feet in length, and from eight to fifteen feet in circumference; they are extremely fat, so that having cut through the skin, which is about an inch in thickness, there is at least a foot of fat before you come to either lean or bones.

Their skins are covered with short grey hair, but their tails and their fins, which serve them for feet on shore, are almost black. They have a distant resemblance to an overgrown seal, though in some particulars there is a manifest difference between them, especially in the males. These have a large snout, or trunk, hanging down five or six inches below the end of the upper jaw, which the females have not.

These animals divide their time equally between the land and the sea, continuing at sea all the summer, and coming on shore at the setting in of winter, where they reside during the whole of that season. In this interval they bring forth their young, and have generally two at a birth, which they suckle with their milk, they being at first about the size of a full-grown seal. During the time these sea-lions continue on shore, they feed on the grass and small plants which grow near the banks of fresh-water streams.

They often, especially the males, have furious battles with each other, principally about their females; and we were one day surprised by the sight of two sea-lions goring each other with their teeth until they were covered with blood.

Anson's Voyage Round the World   Richard Walter

1   Which is the bigger, a sea-lion or a seal?
2   What is the length of a fully grown sea-lion?
3   What is the thickness of a sea-lion's skin?
4   What thickness of fat lies between the skin of a
    sea-lion and its flesh or bones?
5   What purpose is served by the sea-lion's tail and fins
    when it is on shore?
6   Where does the sea-lion spend the summer?
7   Where does it spend the winter?
8   At what time of year are young sea-lions born?
9   How does the face of a male sea-lion differ from that
    of a female?
10   What do the male sea-lions fight about, chiefly?

Contractions

Can't is a short way of writing **cannot**.

I'll is a short way of writing **I will**.

These shortened forms are called **contractions**. Now see how the word **would** is used in contractions.

I would	I'd
she would	she'd
you would	you'd
we would	we'd
he would	he'd
they would	they'd

you would

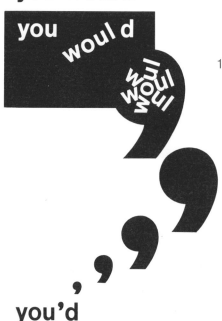

you'd

A In each sentence write a contraction in place of the words in bold type.

1 The police said **they would** be glad of the information.

2 Our teacher asked us if **we would** like to have a concert.

3 I think **you would** be interested in this book.

4 Father said **he would** give me a football next week.

5 Mother promised **she would** help me to swim.

6 The doctor told me **I would** be better in a few days.

B Write the contractions for the following.

1	I am	11	have not
2	you have	12	she will
3	she is	13	I would
4	will not	14	we are
5	he would	15	are not
6	do not	16	you are
7	they are	17	we would
8	shall not	18	they have
9	we have	19	cannot
10	it is	20	they will

C Write the words for which the contractions stand.

1 I **can't** forget that **I'm** bereft
Of all the pleasant sights they see.
The Pied Piper of Hamelin

2 Said Francis then, "Faith, gentlemen, **we're** better here than there."
The Glove and the Lions

3 The old sage said, "**You're** as sound as a nut."
The Enchanted Shirt

4 Out spoke a wife: "**We've** beds at home;
We'll burn them for a light?"
The Wives of Brixham

Antonyms opposites

absent	present
admit	deny
advance	retreat
arrival	departure
bold	timid
cheap	expensive
conceal	reveal
danger	safety
failure	success
false	true
hollow	solid
hurry	loiter
ignorance	knowledge
innocent	guilty
joy	sorrow
miser	spendthrift
permit	forbid
plentiful	scarce
poverty	wealth
proud	humble

A   Write the **opposites** of the following words.

1	joy	7	guilty	13	false
2	miser	8	advance	14	plentiful
3	cheap	9	hollow	15	failure
4	admit	10	arrival	16	poverty
4	permit	11	bold	17	hurry
6	ignorance	12	proud	18	conceal

B   Complete each sentence by inserting the **opposite** of the word in bold type.

1 Mother's new coat was quite **cheap**, but her shoes were very _____ .

2 Nine members were **present** and three were _____ .

3 Some of the defendant's statements were **true**, but many were _____ .

4 The old man was a **miser** but his son turned out to be a _____ .

5 Sally always **hurries** home from school but Carol often _____ on the way.

6 _____ is the curse of God; **knowledge** the wing wherewith we fly to heaven.   *Shakespeare*

C   In each column find the **two antonyms** or opposites.

1	curious	2	plentiful	3	attack
	violent		superior		forbid
	guilty		scarce		receive
	innocent		brilliant		permit
4	timid	5	happiness		
	simple		poverty		
	huge		thrift		
	bold		wealth		

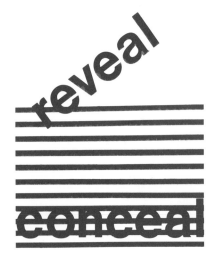

Direct and indirect speech

Direct speech
"Have you cleaned your teeth, Nigel?" asked his mother.

The sentence contains the **exact words** spoken by Nigel's mother.

Direct speech always requires inverted commas, or speech marks, **" "**.

Indirect speech
Nigel's mother asked him if he had cleaned his teeth.

This sentence does not contain the exact words spoken by Nigel's mother.

Indirect speech does not require inverted commas.

A Change to **indirect speech**.

1 "May I have another plum, please Mother?" asked Philip.

2 "I have a bad headache, so I think I will lie down," said Mr. Dean.

3 "The days are certainly getting longer," remarked Mr. Caldwell.

4 "Do you know how to play darts, Roger?" asked David.

5 "You look as if you could do with a good holiday," said Mrs. Smith to her son.

6 "Peter, wash your hands well before coming to the table," said his father.

7 "Come inside, Mrs. Dale," invited the old lady, "and have tea with us."

B Change to **direct speech**.

1 The shoe repairer told Robert that his shoes would be ready by Saturday.

2 Simon's mother asked him if he had loitered on the way home from school.

3 Bernard's teacher asked him if he had ever spent a holiday in France.

4 Bernard replied that he had once spent a month in a villa on the Riviera.

5 The headmaster told the boys that their work was improving.

6 Judith told her father that she had come top in English.

7 Her father exclaimed that he was delighted to see her getting on so well and gave her forty pence.

Compound words

A **compound word** is made up of two or more words.

sign + **post** = **signpost**

Examples
bookstall   toothbrush
matchbox   scarecrow

A   Write the names of the objects in the picture below , showing the two words from which each has been formed.

B   In each of these exercises copy the words in column **a** in the order shown, then add a word from column **b** to form a compound word.

	a	b		a	b
1	wood	pocket	1	saw	wreck
2	post	bare	2	waist	wind
3	pen	snake	3	pass	screen
4	sky	cup	4	speed	piece
5	pick	comb	5	fox	wheel
6	break	knife	6	wind	coat
7	honey	pecker	7	ship	glove
8	rattle	water	8	mantel	dust
9	butter	scraper	9	mill	boat
10	thread	box	10	whirl	port

C   In each line join the two words in bold type, beginning with the second word in each case.

1   a **hole** in a garment through which a **button** goes

2   the **worm** which makes **silk**

3   a **hill** thrown up by a **mole**

4   a sheet of **paper** to which **sand** has been glued

5   the **lights** at the **foot** of a stage

Diminutives

A diminutive is a word representing something small or something young.

Examples

kitten
a young cat

booklet
a small book

bear	cub
cod	codling
deer	fawn
dog	puppy
eagle	eaglet
eel	elver
elephant	calf
frog	tadpole
goose	gosling
hare	leveret
horse	foal
mare	filly
owl	owlet
pig	piglet
river	rivulet
sheep	lamb
stream	streamlet
swan	cygnet
whale	calf

A Write one word for each of the following:

1	a young eel	10	a young cod
2	a baby goose	11	a baby frog
3	a young elephant	12	a young deer
4	a young sheep	13	a young whale
5	a young hare	14	a small river
6	a small stream	15	a young mare
7	a baby owl	16	a young bear
8	a young horse	17	a baby eagle
9	a young dog	18	a young swan

B Write the words which are missing from these sentences.

1 Several tiny _____ followed the eel up the river.

2 The mare and her _____ trotted round the paddock.

3 The _____ and her leverets lay down in the long grass.

4 The _____ and the foal were sold for £900.

5 The _____ and her lamb grazed in the field.

6 The farmer brought the swill for the sow and her six _____ .

7 A swan and her two _____ floated majestically downstream.

8 The cat carried her _____ in her mouth.

The Royal Mint

Hundreds of years ago coins were made in various towns in Britain, including Bristol, Canterbury, London, Winchester and York. After 1810 there was only one Royal Mint, that on Tower Hill, London, but in 1968 a new mint was established at Llantrisant, South Wales, for the manufacture of Britain's decimal currency which was introduced on 15th February 1971.

The metal ingots from which coins are made are melted in closed crucibles for about two hours, and the molten metal is then run into moulds to form coinage-bars which vary in width and thickness according to the coins that are to be made. These bars or strips are next passed between rollers to ensure that they are of uniform size and then put into machines which punch out the blank discs on which the design is to be stamped. After being examined to see that they are of the correct size and shape, these blank discs are fed into annealing drums which soften the metal in preparation for the stamping process. The design is stamped by powerful presses, both sides being done at the same time, and the finished coins are placed on a moving belt for inspection by overlookers who are trained to detect any faults. The newly-minted coins are tested for weight and, after being counted by an automatic machine, are placed in bags, sealed and stored in large strongrooms until required by the banks.

There are no silver coins in Britain's decimal currency, cupro-nickel being used for the 50p, 10p, and 5p pieces.

A sealed bag of 50p pieces contains £250 worth, or 500 coins. Each bag of 10p pieces and 5p pieces contains £100 worth.

1 Name three towns at which coins were made hundreds of years ago.
2 After 1810 there was only one Royal Mint. Where was that?
3 Where was a new Royal Mint established in 1968?
4 When was Britain's decimal currency introduced?
5 How are metal ingots made into coinage-bars?
6 Why are these bars passed between rollers?
7 Why are the blank discs fed into annealing drums?
8 How are the finished coins counted?
9 What metal is used in place of silver for the decimal coins?
10 How many coins would there be in a bag of 5p pieces?

Using the right pronoun

Mistakes are often made in the
use of the pronouns **I** and **me**

Which is correct?	Dad and **me** are going to the football match *or* Dad and **I** are going to the football match.
Make two sentences.	**a** Dad is going to the football match. **b** **I** am going to the football match. **Me** am going to the football match would be wrong.
So the correct sentence is	Dad and **I** are going to the football match.
Which is correct?	Uncle George sent a ticket for Dad and **me** *or* Uncle George sent a ticket for Dad and **I**.
Make two sentences.	**a** Uncle George sent a ticket for Dad. **b** Uncle George sent a ticket for **me**. Uncle George sent a ticket for **I** would be wrong.
So the correct sentence is	Uncle George sent a ticket for Dad and **me**.

After the word **between** always
use the pronoun **me**.

Example
Between you and **I** he can't
afford a new car. (*wrong*)
Between you and **me** he can't
afford a new car. (*right*)

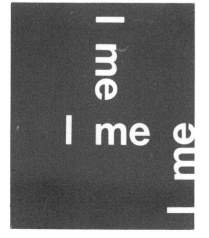

Insert **I** or **me** to complete each sentence.

1 Ann and _____ have won prizes in the drawing
competition.

2 Prizes have been awarded to Ann and _____ .

3 June and _____ have been invited to Barbara's party.

4 Barbara has invited June and _____ to her party.

5 This is a secret between you and _____ .

6 You and _____ must keep this matter secret.

7 The headmaster scolded Robert and _____ for being
so late.

8 Robert and _____ were scolded by the headmaster
for being so late.

9 John and _____ are to share these sweets between
us.

10 These sweets are to be shared between John
and _____ .

Fun with words

A   The second word of each pair is formed from the first word by **changing the first letter**.

1 get   let   2 tree   free   3 bake   take
  game   lame   tour   four   beach   teach
  goose   ____   table   ____   brick   ____

4 shop   chop   5 crow   grow
  slip   clip   clean   glean
  slash   ____   craft   ____

B   The second word of each pair is formed from the first word by **changing the last letter**.

1 cash   cast   2 mare   mark   3 read   ream
  fish   fist   fore   fork   slid   slim
  crush   ____   shrine   ____   hard   ____

4 toe   ton   5 car   cat
  ware   warn   bear   beat
  tore   ____   boar   ____

C   The second word of each pair is formed from the first word by **changing one of the inside letters**.

1 bill   ball   2 stay   sway   3 fast   fist
  pine   pane   store   swore   mane   mine
  firm   ____   stitch   ____   straps   ____

4 meat   moat   5 pale   pane
  lead   load   mile   mine
  beast   ____   bold   ____

D   The second word of each pair is formed from the first word by **inserting a letter immediately after the first letter**.

1 save   shave   2 bow   blow   3 sack   smack
  were   where   fat   flat   sell   smell
  tread   ____   cover   ____   site   ____

4 sip   snip   5 cat   coat
  sore   snore   ram   roam
  gash   ____   vice   ____

Adjectives formation

Many adjectives are formed by adding **-ous** to a word.

Examples

danger**ous**   prosper**ous**
pomp**ous**   riot**ous**

Sometimes spelling changes are made when **-ous** is added.

1 Drop final **e**.
famous   porous
ridiculous   continuous

2 Change **y** to **i**.
furious   injurious
envious

3 Double the last letter.
marvellous   libellous

4 Drop a letter.
humorous   vigorous
glamorous

5 Other changes.
cautious   grievous
miraculous

Atropa Belladonna

POISONOUS

A   Write the missing **adjectives**. When in difficulty consult your dictionary.

1 A substance which is full of pores is ____ .

2 A person who has won fame is ____ .

3 A person who envies others is ____ .

4 A game which is played with vigour is ____ .

5 A room in which there is plenty of space is ____ .

6 A business which prospers is ____ .

7 Berries which poison are ____ .

8 An adventure in which there is peril is ____ .

9 A person who behaves like a villain is ____ .

10 A person who eats like a glutton is ____ .

B   Complete each sentence by using the **adjective** formed from the word in bold type.

1 The Adventures of Tom Sawyer is a ____ story. **humour**

2 The travellers gazed at the ____ scenery. **marvel**

3 The millionaire lives in a ____ house in France. **luxury**

4 The history of Britain is studded with ____ deeds. **glory**

5 When he heard of the retreat the general was ____ . **fury**

6 Paul has always been a ____ boy. **mischief**

7 Hosepipes were turned on the ____ crowd. **riot**

8 The show is ____ from 5.30 to 11 p.m. **continue**

9 Dense fog and smoke are ____ to health. **injury**

10 The crew of the trawler had a ____ escape from death. **miracle**

Proverbs

Learn these proverbs and their meanings, then answer the questions which follow.

A friend in need is a friend indeed.	Whoever helps you when you are in want is a true friend.
Honesty is the best policy.	To be happy, be honest in all your dealings.
A stitch in time saves nine.	Repairs to any damage now will save bigger repairs later.
A rolling stone gathers no moss.	A person who flits from one job to another will never save money.
Strike while the iron is hot.	Carry out your plans when conditions are favourable.
Necessity is the mother of invention.	When something must be done ways and means of doing it will be found.

A

1 What does a stitch in time do?

2 What is the best policy?

3 What is the mother of invention?

4 What does a rolling stone never gather?

B   Write the proverbs containing the following pairs of words. Some are from Book 3.

1	stone	moss	6	strike	iron
2	coat	cloth	7	stitch	time
3	friend	need	8	necessity	invention
4	feathers	birds	9	birds	flock
5	honesty	policy	10	cooks	broth

C   Complete these proverbs.

1 Strike while the ____ is hot.

2 A friend in ____ is a friend indeed.

3 A ____ in time saves nine.

Similes

When something is very **heavy** we say it is **as heavy as lead**.

This is because it is similar to lead in **weight**, although it may be quite different in other ways.

An expression of this kind is called a **simile**.

as sweet as sugar
as bold as brass
as brave as a lion
as bright as a button
as busy as a bee
as clean as a new pin
as cool as a cucumber
as dead as a doornail
as deaf as a doorpost
as fit as a fiddle

What are the missing words?

A

1   as bright as a _____
2   as clean as a _____
3   as deaf as a _____
4   as dead as a _____
5   as brave as a _____
6   as _____ as brass
7   as _____ as a fiddle
8   as _____ as a cucumber
9   as _____ as sugar
10   as _____ as a bee

B   Book 3

1   as fresh as a _____
2   as cunning as a _____
3   as flat as a _____
4   as proud as a _____
5   as quick as _____
6   as _____ as houses
7   as _____ as a feather
8   as _____ as the hills
9   as _____ as a church mouse
10   as _____ as a rock

C   Write the missing words.

1   The old man was as _____ as a doorpost.

2   In walked James as _____ as brass.

3   Old Jacob Marley was as _____ as a doornail.

4   After a hot bath he was as _____ as a new pin.

5   Ann was as busy as a _____ with her knitting.

6   The full-back was as cool as a _____ .

7   Every player in the team was as fit as a _____ .

8   David got up at seven o'clock as bright as a _____ .

Inside the vault

James clutched the edge of the stone step. He said to Arnold "Shall I?" and Arnold told him he'd be a silly idiot not to. He got up, rather slowly, and came forward, and lay down on his stomach and shone the torch down into the hole.

It was smaller than he'd expected. A little, crumbling underground room, with rough masonry walls and rubble all over the floor. And long stone boxes stacked up on top of each other: several at one side, one by itself on the other.

Bert's face appeared at the other side of the hole. "Let's have some light over here."

James swung the torch round. They could see the lettering now on top of the solitary box, black-shadowed in the beam of light. "I thought so," said Bert.

> Here lyeth ye body of
> Thomas Kempe Apothecarie
> he departed this life ye last of October AD 1629
> in the 63 yeare of his Age.

"Apothecary?" said James. His voice dropped into the vault, sounding deep and hollow.

"He couldn't go having them put sorcerer, could he?" said Bert. "Not if he wanted to be in here. The Church wouldn't hold with that."

"Why do you think he wanted to be there?" said James in a whisper. "He wasn't very religious, was he? Believing in all that magic, and hating priests."

The Ghost of Thomas Kempe   Penelope Lively

1   Why was the small room very dark?
2   What were the long stone boxes?
3   On which side of the room was Thomas Kempe's box?
4   Give the day and month of Thomas Kempe's death.
5   In what century did Thomas Kempe die?
6   How old was he when he died?
7   What was his occupation as indicated on the box?
8   What was his true occupation?
9   Why could Thomas Kempe not have his true occupation shown on the box?
10 Say in what two ways he was not a religious man.

Joining sentences

On page 31 we learnt how **conjunctions** are used to join two sentences. This can also be done by using **relative pronouns**.

that
which
who
whom
whose

Example
The policeman spoke to the woman.
Her wallet had been stolen.

The policeman spoke to the woman **whose** wallet had been stolen.

It is possible to join together more than two sentences.

Example
Roger likes English.
He likes arithmetic.
He hates history.

Roger likes English **and** arithmetic **but** hates history.

A   Use one of the words from the list on the left to join each pair of sentences.

1   The police arrested the youth.
He had robbed the bank.

2   Mrs. Baird gave Angela a bracelet.
It was made of gold.

3   The door was opened by a girl.
To her I handed the letter.

4   This is the house.
Jack built it.

5   Sitting near us was a woman.
Her hair had been dyed blue.

B   Write one sentence in place of each group below.

1   The day was cold.
The day was windy.
It was only the first day of February.

2   The dog was barking.
He was trying to get over the gate.
The children kept away from him.

3   The office had closed.
The staff had departed.
It was not yet five o'clock.

4   I had intended to go for a walk.
It started to snow.
I sat by the fire.
I fell fast asleep.

5   Andrew had a bad leg.
He was unable to walk.
He stayed indoors with Gillian.
She read several stories to him.

6   We set off for the woods.
After a while there was a thunderstorm.
We sheltered in an old barn.
It was close at hand.

Abbreviations

Learn the meaning of each of these abbreviations, then answer the questions which follow.

B.S.T.	British Summer Time
C.I.D.	Criminal Investigation Department
e.g.	for example
G.M.T.	Greenwich Mean Time
i.e.	that is
IOU	I owe you
k.o.	knock-out
m.p.g.	miles per gallon
N.B.	Note well
p.a.	per annum (yearly)
Q.C.	Queen's Counsel
R.S.V.P.	Reply if you please
T.B.	Tuberculosis
v.	versus (against)
via	by way of
viz.	namely

A   Write the meaning of each abbreviation in bold type.

1   The ship will sail from Liverpool on July 9th at 14.30 hours **B.S.T.**

2   As he had no money he gave his creditor an **IOU**.

3   The challenger won by a **k.o.** in the ninth round.

4   We travelled from Cardiff to Bristol **via** the Severn Tunnel.

5   Our car will do 40 **m.p.g.** on a long run.

6   His salary is now £8000 **p.a.**

7   Spurs **v.** Dukla was the match of the year.

8   Two officers of the **C.I.D.** arrived at the scene of the crime.

B

1   The ships' clocks were set by **G.M.T.**

2   Prices are drastically reduced, **e.g.** a £300 bed is now priced at £150.

3   At the bottom of the invitation were the letters **R.S.V.P.**

4   He will inherit the money when he is twenty-one, **i.e.** in 1989.

5   **N.B.** All entries must reach this office by May 26th.

6   For years she has suffered from **T.B.**

7   The accused man was defended by Sir Robert John, **Q.C.**

8   There are seven colours in the rainbow, **viz.** red, orange, yellow, green, blue, indigo and violet.

Using the right verb

Learn how these verbs are used, then answer the questions.

to **accede** to a **request**
to **avert** a **catastrophe**
to **contract** a **disease**
to **contradict** a **statement**
to **denounce** an **impostor**
to **disperse** a **mob**
to **estimate** the **cost**
to **evade capture**
to **exterminate pests**
to **impart knowledge**
to **impose** a **fine**
to **inflict punishment**
to **inherit** a **fortune**
to **interpret** a **foreign language**
to **liberate** a **prisoner**
to **prophesy** the **future**
to **redeem** a **promise**
to **reveal** a **secret**
to **surmount** an **obstacle**
to **trespass** on **another's land**

A   Copy and complete these phrases.

1   to _____ a secret
2   to _____ punishment
3   to _____ capture
4   to _____ knowledge
5   to _____ an obstacle
6   to _____ a prisoner
7   to _____ an impostor
8   to _____ the cost
9   to _____ a disease
10 to _____ on another's land
11 to interpret a _____
12 to inherit a _____
13 to disperse a _____
14 to accede to a _____
15 to prophesy the _____
16 to redeem a _____
17 to exterminate _____
18 to avert a _____
19 to contradict a _____
20 to impose a _____

B   Write the verb which will complete each sentence correctly. Use the past tense where required.

1   On his father's death he will _____ a million pounds.

2   The magistrates _____ a fine of £50 and costs.

3   Mounted police were brought in to _____ the demonstrators.

4   The girl who _____ smallpox is seriously ill.

5   A teacher should not only possess knowledge; he should know how to _____ it.

6   There is to be an all-out effort to _____ rabbits on farms.

7   For nearly a month the escaped convict _____ capture.

8   The cost of building the new school is _____ at £6,000,000.

Idioms

In Book 3 you learnt ten sayings which are in common use.

Example

to get into hot water   means to get into trouble

Expressions of this kind are called **idioms**.

Idiom	Meaning
to have an axe to grind	to have something to gain by an action
to be a wet blanket	to be a spoilsport
to draw the long bow	to exaggerate
to make a clean breast of it	to confess to some wrong
to take the bull by the horns	to meet difficulties boldly
to be under a cloud	to be under suspicion
to be a dog in a manger	to deny to others what is useless to oneself
to show the white feather	to show cowardice
to bury the hatchet	to settle a quarrel and live in peace
to flog a dead horse	to do work which produces no results

A   Complete these **idioms** and give the meaning of each.

1   to be under a ___   6   to have an axe ___ ___
2   to flog a ___ horse   7   to take the bull ___ ___ ___
3   to be a dog in a ___   8   to be a wet ___
4   to draw the ___ ___   9   to make a clean ___ ___ ___
5   to bury the ___   10   to show the white ___

B   Rewrite these sentences, substituting the **idiom** for the words in bold type.

1   The detective determined to **meet the difficulties boldly**.

2   Harold told his uncle not to be a **spoilsport**.

3   The old rivals will soon **settle their quarrel and live in peace**.

4   The prefect was **under suspicion** at school.

5   The old sailor is very fond of **exaggerating**.

52

Synonyms similars

abrupt	sudden
accommodation	room
altitude	height
amiable	friendly
brief	short
comprehend	understand
demonstrate	show
diminutive	small
disperse	scatter
eminent	famous
endeavour	try
interior	inside
intoxicated	drunk
invincible	unbeatable
loathe	hate
melancholy	sad
odour	smell
penetrate	pierce
prohibited	forbidden
reluctant	unwilling

A Write a simpler word in place of each word in bold type.

1 Smoking in the factory is **prohibited**.

2 The **odour** of fried sausages came from the kitchen.

3 I read a **brief** report of the accident.

4 We failed to obtain **accommodation** at the hotel.

5 This year our cricket team has proved **invincible**.

6 He was most **reluctant** to leave home.

7 We will **endeavour** to deliver the goods today.

8 Mounted police were sent to **disperse** the large crowd.

9 The plane was flying at an **altitude** of 10,000 metres.

10 Our train came to an **abrupt** stop.

B In each group below select the word which is similar in meaning to the word in bold type.

1 **eminent**

handsome
skilful
famous

2 **intoxicated**

drunk
unconscious
sober

3 **comprehend**

fear
understand
pretend

4 **loathe**

hate
adore
respect

5 **demonstrate**

fight
squander
show

6 **interior**

cheap
inside
common

7 **amiable**

rude
stout
friendly

8 **melancholy**

sad
jolly
greedy

9 **penetrate**

thicken
pierce
collapse

10 **diminutive**

tough
dark
small

53

A pony for Jody

Jody could begin to see things now. He looked into the box stall and then stepped back quickly.

A red pony colt was looking at him out of the stall. Its tense ears were forward and a light of disobedience was in its eyes. Its coat was rough and thick as an Airedale's fur and its mane was long and tangled. Jody's throat collapsed in on itself and cut his breath short.

"He needs a good currying," his father said, "and if I ever hear of you not feeding him or leaving his stall dirty I'll sell him off in a minute."

Jody couldn't bear to look at the pony's eyes any more. He gazed down at his hands for a moment, and he asked very shyly: "Mine?" No one answered him. He put his hand out toward the pony. Its grey nose came close, sniffing loudly, and then the lips drew back and the strong teeth closed on Jody's fingers. The pony shook its head up and down and seemed to laugh with amusement. Jody regarded his bruised fingers. "Well," he said with pride – "well, I guess he can bite all right." The two men laughed, somewhat in relief. Carl Tiflin went out of the barn and walked up a side-hill to be by himself, for he was embarrassed, but Billy Buck stayed. It was easier to talk to Billy Buck. Jody asked again – "Mine?"

Billy became professional in tone. "Sure! That is, if you look out for him and break him right. I'll show you how. He's just a colt. You can't ride him for some time."

The Red Pony   John Steinbeck

1 Why did Jody step back from the box stall?
2 Which two words indicate the pony's mood and attitude?
3 Why did Jody's throat "collapse in on itself"?
4 What two things did Jody's father warn him he must do?
5 Why couldn't he bear to look at the pony's eye any more?
6 Why did Jody speak of the pony with pride?
7 Why were the two men relieved as they laughed?
8 Why did Carl Tiflin want to be by himself?
9 Why could the pony not be ridden for some time?
10 Who was going to help Jody break in the pony?

Occupations

A Write the names of these occupations.

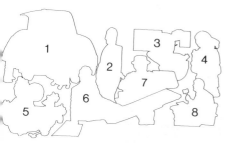

architect fishmonger
auctioneer florist
author mechanic
caddie reporter
chauffeur sculptor
dentist solicitor
detective

B Write the missing occupations.

1 The _____ sorted out the difficult legal case.

2 The keen _____ was at the airport to meet the famous actress.

3 The _____ has finished drawing the plans of the school.

4 A _____ and two policemen soon arrived at the scene of the crime.

5 The flowers for the wedding were supplied by the local _____ .

6 I bought some cod and plaice from the _____ .

7 The _____ knocked the piano down at ninety pounds.

8 This is the largest statue the _____ has ever made.

9 The _____ had no difficulty in discovering what was wrong with the car.

C What name is given to a person who:

1 carries a golfer's clubs?
2 sells flowers and plants?
3 writes books and stories?
4 drives his employer's car?
5 examines and repairs teeth?

55

Sentence structure

Let me know when you are ready.

When you are ready let me know.

Both these sentences contain exactly the same words, although not in the same order.

A   Rewrite each sentence below, using the same words, but commencing with the word in bold type.

1   Julia persisted in talking **although** she had been warned not to do so.

2   She ordered the dress **without** thinking how she could pay for it.

3   Two sailors were having an argument **on** the quay.

4   The convict was recaptured **just** as night was falling.

5   The express train rushed into the tunnel **with** a shriek of its whistle.

6   You will be seriously ill **if** you do not check that cough.

7   A huge log fire blazed **in** the great hall of the castle.

8   The girl was up and about **long** before daybreak.

a   A rattlesnake **bit** the lumberjack.

b   The lumberjack **was bitten** by a rattlesnake.

Both these sentences convey the same idea, but the words they contain are not exactly the same.

(**a**) contains the word **bit**, the Past Tense of bite.

(**b**) contains the word **bitten**, the Past Participle of bite.

B   Rewrite these sentences, beginning with the word in bold type in each case, and making such changes as are necessary.

1   Charles Dickens wrote **A** Christmas Carol.

2   The Rovers beat **the** Wanderers 2-0 last Saturday.

3   A gang of thieves stole **the** valuable portrait.

4   The County Architect drew **the** plans of the dining-hall.

5   The heavy fall shook **the** frail old gentleman.

6   The twins took **Spot** to the park.

7   Our puppy tore **that** curtain.

8   The three girls chose **the** curtains for the lounge.

Alphabetical order

A Arrange the words in each group in alphabetical order. Look at the **fifth** letter of each word.

1	straw	2	handicap	3	catapult
	strap		handy		catastrophe
	straight		handsome		catalogue
	stray		handle		catacomb
	strand		handful		cataract

4	fortress	5	partner	6	compile
	fortunate		partly		complain
	fortify		partake		compel
	forth		party		compose
	fortnight		partial		compare

This is a drawing of a ten-volume encyclopaedia. Each volume is numbered and also shows the first four letters of the first word and the last word it contains.

A to BALL — VOLUME 1
BALM to CARF — VOLUME 2
CARG to DELI — VOLUME 3
DELL to FOYN — VOLUME 4
FRAC to HUNS — VOLUME 5
HUNT to LOGG — VOLUME 6
LOGI to NORI — VOLUME 7
NORM to RHET — VOLUME 8
RHEU to SUCC — VOLUME 9
SUCH to ZYWI — VOLUME 10

B Give the numbers of the volumes in which you would look for the following words.

1	longitude	8	athletics	15	foundry
2	Dunlop	9	portcullis	16	decimal
3	meteor	10	Henry VIII	17	resin
4	indigo	11	Kiel Canal	18	Napoleon
5	cardinal	12	gannet	19	shorthand
6	balsa	13	vodka	20	crypt
7	tambourine	14	Jolly Roger		

Adjectives formation

Noun	Adjective
athlete	athletic
benefit	beneficial
circle	circular
credit	creditable
custom	customary
effect	effective
energy	energetic
fire	fiery
fraud	fraudulent
giant	gigantic
influence	influential
metal	metallic
method	methodical
muscle	muscular
nonsense	nonsensical
picture	picturesque
science	scientific
skill	skilful
sympathy	sympathetic
system	systematic

A　Form **adjectives** from these nouns.

1	muscle	7	skill	13	science
2	effect	8	benefit	14	fire
3	fraud	9	system	15	picture
4	athlete	10	credit	16	influence
5	sympathy	11	method	17	circle
6	energy	12	giant	18	metal

B　Write the missing **adjectives**.

1　an ___ remedy　**effect**

2　a ___ craftsman　**skill**

3　a ___ sound　**metal**

4　an ___ man　**athlete**

5　a ___ age　**science**

6　a ___ saw　**circle**

7　an ___ worker　**energy**

8　a ___ holiday　**benefit**

9　a ___ reply　**nonsense**

10　a ___ friend　**sympathy**

11　a ___ scene　**picture**

12　a ___ scheme　**fraud**

C　Complete each sentence by inserting the **adjective** formed from the noun in bold type.

1　Police made a ___ search of the building. **system**

2　The scientist is noted for his ___ work.　**method**

3　Paul's success was a most ___ achievement. **credit**

4　The key was not in its ___ place.　**custom**

5　We stayed at a ___ Cornish fishing village. **picture**

Capital letters

Capital letters are used for:

names of persons
pets
days
months *but not seasons*
special holidays
geographical names
nations
languages
titles of books, poems, songs, etc.

A Rewrite these sentences, using capital letters where necessary.

1 the river thames is sometimes referred to as old father thames.

2 both german and italian are taught at grosvenor grammar school.

3 rudyard kipling, who was born in india, wrote many fine books, the most famous being the jungle books.

4 easter is a movable festival which may come in march or april, but christmas is not.

5 the bank of england is sometimes called the old lady of threadneedle street.

6 linda's brother colin is a patient at the middlesex hospital.

7 the white tower in the tower of london was built by gundulf, bishop of rochester, about A.D. 1078.

8 from monday to friday the shop closes at 5.30; on saturdays it closes at 1 o'clock.

B Copy these sentences and insert punctuation marks in each.

1 Would you like to tour Europe and see its wonderful sights

2 In the market there were ample supplies of apples pears oranges bananas peaches and grapes

3 James did you give my message to the headmaster asked his mother

4 Yes Mother I gave it to him before lessons began replied James

5 Some members wont be present but it doesnt matter

6 The ticket bore the date Thurs 26th Sept in bold type

7 The bat we played with was Toms but the ball was Duncans.

8 Oh dear exclaimed Miss Taylor in alarm I have lost my purse

Encounter with a dinosaur

Something was swimming toward the lighthouse tower.

It was a cold night, as I have said; the high tower was cold, the light coming and going, and the Fog Horn calling and calling through the ravelling mist. You couldn't see far and you couldn't see plain, but there was the deep sea moving on its way about the night earth, flat and quiet, the colour of grey mud, and here were the two of us alone in the high tower, and there, far out at first, was a ripple, followed by a wave, a rising, a bubble, a bit of froth. And then, from the surface of the cold sea came a head, a large head, dark-coloured, with immense eyes, and then a neck. And then – not a body – but more neck and more! The head rose a full forty feet above the water on a slender and beautiful dark neck. Only then did the body, like a little island of black coral and shells and crayfish, drip up from the subterranean. There was a flicker of tail. In all, from head to tail, I estimated the monster at ninety or a hundred feet.

I don't know what I said. I said something.

"Steady, boy, steady," whispered McDunn.

"It's impossible!" I said.

"No, Johnny, *we're* impossible. *It's* like it always was ten million years ago. It hasn't changed. It's *us* and the land that've changed, become impossible. *Us!*"

It swam slowly and with a great dark majesty out in the icy waters, far away. The fog came and went about it, momentarily erasing its shape.

The Fog Horn   Ray Bradbury

1   On what kind of night did this story take place?
2   What sound could be heard?
3   How much visibility was there?
4   Which movement first told the men there was something in the sea?
5   Where did the men first see this movement?
6   At what height above the water did the head rise?
7   To what does the writer compare the monster's body?
8   How long was the monster?
9   When did McDunn suggest these monsters had once lived?
10 Why was the monster not continuously visible?

Homophones

herd	a number of animals together
heard	past tense of hear
key	locks a door, etc.
quay	a landing-place for ships
night	time between evening and morning
knight	a titled gentleman
muscle	part of the body
mussel	a shellfish
place	a particular part of space
plaice	a flat-fish
profit	gain; benefit
prophet	one who foretells events
sew	to work with needle and thread
sow	to scatter seed
stile	steps in a fence or wall
style	fashion
vale	a valley
veil	thin material covering the face
stationery	writing materials
stationary	standing still

A Choose the correct word from the pair above to complete each sentence.

1 **vale   veil**
The bride wore a ＿＿ of lace.

2 **stationery   stationary**
The fast sports car collided with a ＿＿ saloon car.

3 **profit   prophet**
The ＿＿ foretold the defeat of the Hebrews.

4 **sow   sew**
In spring farmers plough their fields and ＿＿ the seed.

5 **muscle   mussel**
Having pulled a ＿＿ in his thigh the centre-half had to leave the field.

B Complete each sentence by using a suitable pair of homophones from your list.

1 The thundering hoofs of the stampeding ＿＿ of buffalo could be ＿＿ from a long way off.

2 The ＿＿ to the sailor's chest was found lying on the ＿＿ .

3 The black ＿＿ rode out one ＿＿ to attack the baron's castle.

4 The athlete vaulted over the ＿＿ in fine ＿＿ .

5 The fishmonger put the huge ＿＿ in a prominent ＿＿ on the marble slab.

Twin words

Many common English expressions consist of two simple words joined by the word **and**.

Learn the expressions in this list. Exercise B shows you how these expressions are used.

flesh and blood
heart and soul
long and short
short and sweet
there and then
thick and thin
tooth and nail
touch and go
ups and downs
ways and means
wear and tear
well and good

A   Copy these expressions and insert the missing words.

1 thick and ____
2 ____ and go
3 there and ____
4 ____ and tear
5 flesh and ____
6 ____ and means
7 long and ____
8 ____ and nail
9 heart and ____
10 ____ and good
11 ups and ____
12 ____ and sweet

B   Write the words needed to complete these sentences.

1 We must consider ways and ____ of building a school swimming bath.

2 The tramp's clothes showed signs of much wear and ____ .

3 The patient recovered from the operation but it was touch and ____ .

4 The discontented film star left the studio ____ and then.

5 The financier had seen many ____ and downs in his life.

6 A loyal friend sticks to you through ____ and thin.

7 The old man had little affection for his own ____ and blood.

8 If you are prepared to accept the responsibility all well and ____ .

9 The cornered men fought tooth and ____ before they surrendered.

10 A person whose heart and ____ is in his work puts all his energy into it.

Rhymes

farms
be
floors
rye
roars
tower
I
arms
see
devour
doors
sails
me
flails
flour

A   Write the words, numbered 1 to 15, which fill the spaces in the verses below.

Behold! a giant am ____   1
Aloft here in my ____ . 2
With my granite jaws I ____   3
The maize, and the wheat and the ____ , 4
And grind them into ____ . 5

I look down over the ____   6
In the fields of grain I ____   7
The harvest that is to ____ , 8
And I fling to the air my ____   9
For I know it is all for ____ . 10

I hear the sound of ____   11
Far off, from the threshing ____ , 12
In barns, with their open ____ , 13
And the wind, the wind in my ____   14
Louder and louder ____ . 15

B   Write the word needed to complete each sentence. In each case the missing word rhymes with the word in bold type.

1   He was sorry to have to ____ the invitation.   **fine**

2   She will ____ her hundredth birthday tomorrow.
wait

3   The architect will ____ the site for the school.   **play**

4   The rabbit was caught in a ____ .   **pair**

5   The ____ against smoking will receive strong support.   **main**

6   Wise parents rarely ____ in the quarrels of their children.   **deer**

7   When you pay a bill you should obtain a ____ .
meet

8   ____ furniture is very old and often very valuable.
beak

9   We are going to ____ our parts for the school play.
purse

10   The tourists stayed at a ____ village in the Alps.
desk

Prepositions

The dog is **on** the chair.

The dog is **under** the table.

The dog is **in** the car.

The words **in**, **under** and **on** show how the word 'dog' is related to the words **car**, **table** and **chair**.

A word which shows the relationship between a noun (or pronoun) and some other word in a sentence is called a preposition.

after	from
against	off
along	on
around	outside
before	through

A   Insert the prepositions in the list on the left in their correct places in the sentences which follow.

1   Judith is suffering _____ influenza.

2   Crowds of people strolled _____ the promenade.

3   Grandpa was seated _____ a blazing fire.

4   Henry leaned _____ the wall of the gymnasium.

5   The dog ran _____ the cat, but could not catch it.

6   Drake was the first Englishman to sail _____ the world.

7   The circus dog jumped right _____ the hoop.

8   A long queue formed _____ the football ground.

9   Lovely water lilies floated _____ the surface of the pond.

10   A workman fell _____ a ladder and was badly hurt.

Using prepositions correctly

between	Things are shared between two persons.
among	Things are shared among more than two.
in	Shows position in one place. *e.g.* The budgie was in its cage.
into	Shows movement from one place to another. *e.g.* The budgie hopped from the table into its cage.
differ	The twins differ **from** each other in some ways. I beg to differ **with** you on that point.
different	This book is quite different **from** the one I read last. (Never use **to** or **than** with different.)

beside	Means by the side of.
	e.g. Simon sits beside me in school.
besides	Means in addition to.
	e.g. Another bicycle was stolen besides John's.

Note that the same word may be followed by different prepositions.

Examples

a   I agree **with** you in everything you say.
I hope you will agree **to** my suggestion.

b   The headmaster was angry **with** the children.
He was angry **at** their bad behaviour.

c   The soldier died **for** his country.
The soldier died **of** wounds.

d   The traveller lives **in** Bournemouth.
He lives **at** 27 Broad Street.

e   He would not part **with** a penny.
She hates to part **from** her mother.

B   Use a **preposition** to complete each sentence.

1   The children were walking about _____ the classroom.

2   The children went from the playground _____ the classroom.

3   Do you agree _____ this proposal?

4   He will agree _____ everything you say.

5   The prize was divided _____ the two winners.

6   The prize was divided _____ several competitors.

7   Angus now lives _____ Edinburgh.

8   He lives with his aunt _____ 49 Argyll Street.

9   The matron stood _____ the patient's bed.

10   He has a private income _____ his large salary.

C   Use these phrases in sentences of your own.

1	walked in	5	walked behind
2	walked into	6	walked under
3	walked on	7	walked through
4	walked across	8	walked round

Tarka fights Deadlock

Between boulders and rocks crusted with shellfish and shaggy with seaweed, past worm-channelled posts that marked the fairway for fishing boats at high water, the pack hunted the otter. Off each post a gull launched itself, cackling angrily as it looked down at the animals. Tarka reached the sea. He walked slowly into the surge of a wavelet, and sank away from the chop of old Harper's jaws, just as Deadlock ran through the pack. Hounds swam beyond the line of waves, while people stood at the sea-lap and watched the huntsman wading to his waist. It was said that the otter was dead-beat, and probably floating stiffly in the shallow water. After a few minutes the huntsman shook his head, and withdrew the horn from his waistcoat. He filled his lungs and stopped his breath and was tightening his lips for the four long notes of the call-off, when a brown head with hard dark eyes, was thrust out of the water a yard from Deadlock. Tarka stared into the hound's face and cried "Ic-yang".

The head sank. Swimming under Deadlock, Tarka bit on to the loose skin of the flews and pulled the hound's head under the water. Deadlock tried to twist round and crush the otter's skull in his jaws, but he struggled vainly. Bubbles blew out of his mouth. Soon he was choking. The hounds did not know what was happening. Deadlock's hindlegs kicked the air weakly. The huntsman waded out and pulled him inshore, but Tarka loosened his bite only when he needed new air in his lungs.

Tarka the Otter   Henry Williamson

1   Name three physical features that were part of the shore where the otter was hunted.
2   What made the gulls angry?
3   What were the people standing on the shore doing?
4   What did people think had happened to Tarka?
5   Why did the huntsman shake his head?
6   What did he then prepare to do?
7   What prevented him from performing this action?
8   Why was Deadlock's struggle in vain?
9   What part of Deadlock's body was above the surface of the water?
10 Why did Tarka loosen his bite?

Containers

A **caddy** is a container for **tea**. A **purse** is a container for **money**.

A Write the names of the containers shown in the pictures.

B Write in order the words which have been omitted from these sentences.

barrel	quiver
caddy	rucksack
chest	safe
crate	satchel
cupboard	scabbard
dustbin	scuttle
holster	sheath
kitbag	vase
manger	wallet
purse	wardrobe

1   The carpenter's tools were kept in a large wooden ____ .

2   The china was packed in straw in a large ____ .

3   Penelope poured the contents of two packets of tea into the ____ .

4   There are piles of plates in the kitchen ____ .

5   Sarah hung her best dress in her mother's ____ .

6   The cowboy put his revolver back in its ____ .

7   The archer took an arrow from his ____ .

8   Many walkers carry a ____ on their backs.

9   The ____ in Black Beauty's stable was piled up with hay.

10   Farmer Giles gave the haymakers a ____ of cider.

Words with more than one meaning

Some words have more than one meaning.

Example
You should **check** the working of every sum.
The bookmaker wore a **check** suit.

charge	litter
chest	plane
coach	spring
express	stern
ground	temple

11 . 12

A   Write the numbers from 1 to 10 in a column, then opposite each write the word which will complete both sentences.

1   The beach was covered with ＿＿ after the vast crowd of holiday-makers had left.
Trixie had a ＿＿ of six lovely puppies.

2   The carpenter kept his tools in a wooden ＿＿ .
A cold on the ＿＿ often makes breathing difficult.

3   The ＿＿ for admission to the circus was £1.
The troops were ordered to ＿＿ the enemy.

4   He could not find words to ＿＿ his thanks.
The ＿＿ train was travelling at 150 kilometres an hour.

5   The ＿＿ was covered with fallen leaves.
The coffee was ＿＿ by machinery.

6   The daffodil is my favourite ＿＿ flower.
The ＿＿ of the clock was broken.

7   A ＿＿ man is very strict and severe.
The ＿＿ of a ship is the rear part.

8   Carpenters ＿＿ wood to make it smooth.
The ＿＿ circled the airport twice before landing.

9   Several Hindus were worshipping in the ＿＿ .
A blow on the ＿＿ rendered the man unconscious.

10   A new master had been appointed to ＿＿ the boys at cricket.
The motor ＿＿ was carrying thirty-five passengers on a school journey.

B   Use your dictionary to find six words which have more than one meaning. Write sentences to show the different meanings.

Occupations

A   Write the names of these occupations.

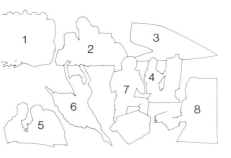

B   Choose the word in your list which will complete each of these sentences correctly.

1   When the ____ had finished stuffing and mounting the barn owl it looked very lifelike.

2   People who travel in foreign countries often need an ____ to make themselves understood.

3   An exhibition of paintings by a local ____ was held in the town hall.

4   She is a trained ____ specializing in skin care.

5   The ____ was forced to make a crash landing.

6   A number of experienced ____ were consulted about the new bridge.

7   The ____ told the magistrates that his client had been assaulted by the defendant.

8   The ____ collected the tickets at the booking office.

9   He has arthritis and is treated by a ____ each week.

10 The ____ performed the heart transplant successfully.

artist
actress
ballerina
beautician
chiropodist
conjurer
engineer
interpreter
juggler
lumberjack

messenger
optician
photographer
physiotherapist
pilot
solicitor
surgeon
taxidermist
teacher
ventriloquist

Antonyms opposites

ancient	modern
ascend	descend
attack	defence
captivity	freedom
cautious	reckless
coarse	fine
compulsory	voluntary
defeat	victory
entrance	exit
expand	contract
exterior	interior
famine	glut
import	export
increase	decrease
inferior	superior
majority	minority
maximum	minimum
permanent	temporary
punishment	reward
transparent	opaque

A What are the **opposites** of the following words?

1	expand	10	inferior
2	victory	11	entrance
3	maximum	12	transparent
4	famine	13	cautious
5	coarse	14	descend
6	increase	15	import
7	punishment	16	permanent
8	majority	17	exterior
9	captivity	18	compulsory

B Copy and complete each sentence by inserting the **opposite** of the word in bold type.

1 Both the ____ and the **exit** of the building were well lighted.

2 This file is too ____ ; try a **fine** one.

3 During his long service the general had known both ____ and **defeat**.

4 Service with the Armed Forces was ____ for men and **voluntary** for women.

5 The castle is an ____ building, but the church is quite **modern**.

6 The ____ of the house needs painting but the **interior** is perfect.

7 The team is strong in ____ but weak in **defence**.

8 **Cautious** motorists often have to suffer for the folly of the ____ .

9 After two years of ____ the prisoners of war thought **freedom** was wonderful.

10 The teacher believed in ____ for the wicked and **reward** for the good.

People

eavesdropper	Listens to conversations not intended for his ears.
emigrant	Leaves his own country to settle in another.
immigrant	Comes into a country and makes his home there.
impostor	Tries to make people think that he is somebody else.
optimist	Always looks on the bright side of life.
pessimist	Looks on the gloomy side of life.
scapegoat	Takes the blame for the misdoings of others.
stowaway	Hides in a ship or plane to avoid paying the fare.
vegetarian	Eats no meat; has fruit, vegetables.
wiseacre	Claims to be very wise.

A   Write one word for each of the following.

1   A man who thinks he knows the answer to every question.

2   A person who accepts the blame for a wrong done by another.

3   A person who listens at keyholes.

4   A person who believes that every cloud has a silver lining.

5   A man who goes about posing as a famous general.

B   Use one word from the list to complete each sentence.

1   Being a born ＿＿ , Bailey could not help taking a gloomy view of the matter.

2   The ＿＿ was discovered hiding in a hold of the ship.

3   The ＿＿ waved farewell to his relatives as his ship drew away from the quay.

4   Finding meat injurious to his health he decided to become a ＿＿ .

5   The ＿＿ was caught in the act of listening at the keyhole of the manager's door.

Gerard and the bear

Gerard looked wildly down. He was forty feet from the
ground. Death below. Death moving slowly but surely upon
him in a still more horrible form. The bear crawled on; he saw
its open jaws and bloodshot eyes. Hearing a twang he glanced
down, and saw Denys shooting up at the bear. The animal
snarled at the twang, but crawled on. Again the crossbow
twanged, and the next moment the bear was close upon
Gerard, who sat on the branch, paralysed. The bear opened
her jaws and hot blood spouted from them upon Gerard as
from a pump. The bough rocked. The wounded monster was
reeling; it stuck its sickles of claws deep into the wood; it
toppled, its claws held firm, but its body rolled off, and the
sudden shock to the branch shook Gerard forward on his
stomach with his face upon one of the bear's straining paws.
At this she raised her head up, up, till he felt her hot breath.
Then huge teeth snapped together loudly close below him,
with a last effort of baffled hate. The ponderous body rent the
claws out of the bough, then pounded the earth with a
tremendous thump. There was a shout of triumph below, and
then a cry of dismay, for Gerard had fainted, and had rolled
headlong from the perilous height.

    Denys caught at Gerard, and somewhat checked his fall;
but it is doubtful whether this alone would have saved him
from breaking his neck or a limb. His best friend now was the
dying bear, on whose hairy body his head and shoulders safely
fell.

The Cloister and the Hearth   Charles Reade

1 How high above the ground was the branch on
    which Gerard sat?
2 Who was standing beneath this tree?
3 What caused the "twang" which Gerard heard?
4 What did the bear do when she heard this noise?
5 What happened when the bear opened her jaws?
6 Which word tells us that Gerard was unable to
    move?
7 How was the bear able to cling to the branch
    although its body had toppled over?
8 What effect did the sudden shock caused by the
    bear rolling off the branch have upon Gerard?
9 Why was there a cry of dismay from below?
10 Why was the dying bear Gerard's best friend when
     fell from the branch of the tree?

Agreement of subject and verb

The **subject** of a sentence must agree with its **verb** in number.

A **singular subject** requires a **singular verb**.

Example
A **cow is** a very useful animal.

A **plural subject** requires a **plural verb**.

Example
Cows are very useful animals.

Now look carefully at this sentence.

A fine **selection** of used cars **was** on view.

The noun **selection**, which is the **subject**, is **singular**, so the singular verb **was** must be used.

Always use a **singular verb** with **each**, **anybody**, **nobody**, **everybody**, **everyone**, **no one**, **either**, **neither**.

Example
Neither of these knives **is** very sharp.

A Choose the correct **verb** from the pair above to complete each sentence.

1 **has**   **have**
A violet ____ a fragrant smell.

2 **has**   **have**
Violets ____ a fragrant smell.

3 **wasn't**   **weren't**
The book ____ on the shelf.

4 **wasn't**   **weren't**
The books ____ on the shelf.

5 **tries**   **try**
The boys ____ hard to make good progress.

6 **tries**   **try**
The boy ____ hard to make good progress.

B Watch for the **subject** in each sentence and use the verb which agrees with it in number.

1 **has**   **have**
One of the twins ____ very red hair.

2 **has**   **have**
Both of the twins ____ rosy cheeks.

3 **was**   **were**
The bunch of keys ____ lost in the street.

4 **was**   **were**
The keys ____ lost in the street.

5 **makes**   **make**
A box of chocolates ____ a nice present.

6 **makes**   **make**
Chocolates ____ a nice present.

7 **is**   **are**
Road accidents ____ increasing in number.

8 **is**   **are**
The number of road accidents ____ increasing.

9 **gives**   **give**
Flowers ____ many people great pleasure.

10 **gives**   **give**
A bunch of flowers ____ many people pleasure.

Similes

Learn this list of similes, then work the exercises.

as happy as a lark
as mad as a hatter
as meek as a lamb
as patient as Job
as pleased as Punch
as proud as a peacock
as right as rain
as silent as the grave
as slippery as an eel
as smooth as velvet

Complete these similes.

A

1 as right as ____
2 as silent as the ____
3 as pleased as ____
4 as slippery as an ____
5 as happy as a ____
6 as ____ as velvet
7 as ____ as a lamb
8 as ____ as a hatter
9 as ____ as Job
10 as ____ as a peacock

B Revision

1 as cool as a ____
2 as fit as a ____
3 as busy as a ____
4 as deaf as a ____
5 as brave as a ____
6 as ____ as brass
7 as ____ as a new pin
8 as ____ as a doornail
9 as ____ as a button
10 as ____ as sugar

C Write the missing words.

1 Although her children are often naughty, Mrs. Jones is as patient as ____ .

2 Jane's skin is as smooth as ____ .

3 At night most villages are as silent as the ____ .

4 David had to shout loudly because the old man was as deaf as a ____ .

5 The full-back was dazed by the tackle, but after receiving attention from the trainer he was as right as ____ .

6 Martin is as happy as a ____ when playing with his electric railway.

7 Philip was as pleased as ____ with his examination results.

8 The prisoner was as meek as a ____ when he faced the judge.

74

Words which save work

One word can sometimes do the work of several.

Example

People who eat more than is good for them are rarely healthy.

Gluttons are rarely healthy.

accidentally
apologized
author
drought
fearlessly
immediately
librarian
occasionally
postponed
recently
revolved
speechless
surrendered
survivors
talkative

A   In each sentence below, replace the words in bold type with a labour-saving word from the list on the left.

1   I met Robert in London **not long ago**.

2   The rebel leader **gave himself up** to the Government forces.

3   Owing to bad weather the school sports had to be **put off to a later date**.

4   Gillian is a bright pupil but rather **fond of talking too much**.

5   After his surprise win Roger was **incapable of speaking**.

6   It is wise to visit the dentist **every now and then**.

7   The **great shortage of rain** has ruined the crops.

8   Of the forty-two passengers in the plane crash, there were only three **who remained alive**.

B

1   The window was broken **by accident**.

2   The hooligans were ordered to leave the cinema **without further delay**.

3   I received a copy of the book of poems from the **man who wrote it**.

4   The policeman tackled the armed robber **without any fear**.

5   Robert asked the **man in charge of the library** if he could recommend the book he had chosen.

6   The chairman of the meeting **expressed his regret** for his late arrival.

7   The blades of the electric fan **turned round and round** at a fantastic speed.

Homophones

bail	**a** money paid to set a person free
	b crosspiece of a wicket
bale	a large bundle
berth	place to sleep on a ship
birth	being born
faint	**a** condition like sleep or death
	b weak; not plain
feint	a sham blow or attack
gilt	thin covering of gold
guilt	state of having done wrong
stake	a pointed stick
steak	a slice of meat or fish
lessen	to grow or make less
lesson	something learnt or taught
root	underground part of a plant
route	a way to go; a road
sight	power or act of seeing
site	position or place
soar	to fly upwards or at a great height
sore	painful
hoard	to save and store up
horde	a crowd, e.g. of hooligans

From the list on the left, choose the correct homophone to complete each sentence.

1 We watched the skylark ＿＿ up into the sky.

2 The champion made a ＿＿ with his left then landed with a punishing right hook.

3 Two of the accused men were released on ＿＿ .

4 Our new house is being built on a sunny ＿＿ .

5 On the voyage to America Tony slept on an upper ＿＿ .

6 The prisoner admitted his ＿＿ and was sentenced to three months imprisonment.

7 No sooner had he scored a goal than he was surrounded by a ＿＿ of hooligans.

8 A strong ＿＿ was driven into the earth to support the young apple tree.

9 The tablets he took did much to ＿＿ the pain in his chest.

10 Before we began our tour, Father planned the ＿＿ we were to take.

Noises of creatures

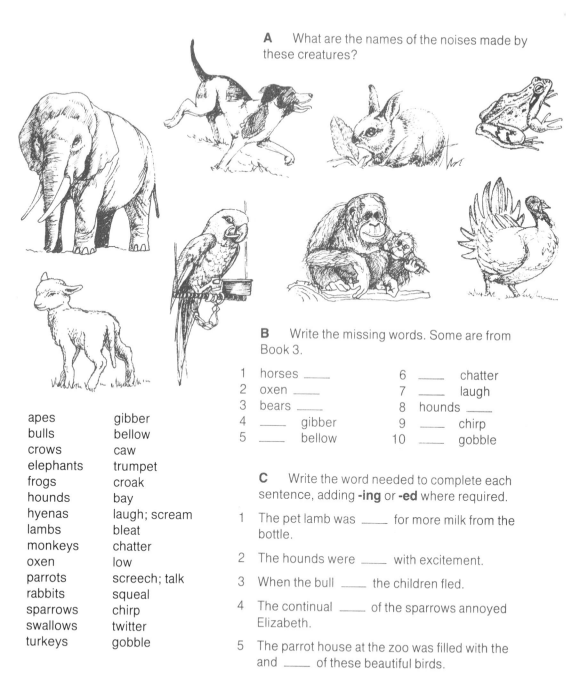

A What are the names of the noises made by these creatures?

apes	gibber
bulls	bellow
crows	caw
elephants	trumpet
frogs	croak
hounds	bay
hyenas	laugh; scream
lambs	bleat
monkeys	chatter
oxen	low
parrots	screech; talk
rabbits	squeal
sparrows	chirp
swallows	twitter
turkeys	gobble

B Write the missing words. Some are from Book 3.

1 horses ____   6 ____ chatter
2 oxen ____   7 ____ laugh
3 bears ____   8 hounds ____
4 ____ gibber   9 ____ chirp
5 ____ bellow   10 ____ gobble

C Write the word needed to complete each sentence, adding **-ing** or **-ed** where required.

1 The pet lamb was ____ for more milk from the bottle.

2 The hounds were ____ with excitement.

3 When the bull ____ the children fled.

4 The continual ____ of the sparrows annoyed Elizabeth.

5 The parrot house at the zoo was filled with the and ____ of these beautiful birds.

6 Judy, the elephant, ____ expectantly as her keeper approached with the food.

7 The old frog ____ contentedly as he hopped about on the edge of the pond.

Katy's narrow escape

It wasn't easy for Katy to stand still while her aunt was sewing the string on her bonnet, and now and then, in a moment of forgetfulness sticking the needle into one's chin. Katy bore it as well as she could, but the moment she was released she rushed to the gate, where little Clover stood waiting patiently.

"We shall have to run," gasped Katy, "or we shall be late." So they ran as fast as they could, but before they were half-way to school the town clock struck nine and all hope was over. This vexed Katy very much for she was always eager to be early, and she marched into school in a very cross mood.

But as soon as the recess bell rang she hurried into the playground and climbed onto the roof of the wood-shed. Suddenly a gust of wind blew her bonnet into the playground of Miller's School next-door. In another minute the Miller girls would be out. Already she imagined them dancing round her bonnet, pinning it on a pole, using it as a football and waving it over the fence. . . .

So sliding rapidly down the roof Katy vaulted over the fence into the Miller playground, but just then the Miller recess bell tinkled and a little Millerite squeaked out to the others, "There's Katy Carr in our playground." With a howl of fury they hurled themselves on Katy, but she . . . was already half-way up the fence. . . . Just as she went over a Millerite seized her by the last foot. With a frantic kick Katy released herself, and her assailant fell head over heels backwards, while with a shriek of triumph and fright she plunged into a group of her friends who stood transfixed at the astonishing sight of one of their number returning alive from the enemy camp.

What Katy Did   Susan Coolidge

1   What did Katy's aunt do now and then when sewing the bonnet?
2   What did Katy do the moment she was released by her aunt?
3   Why was Katy in such a hurry?
4   What was Katy's mood as she marched into school?
5   What did Katy do as soon as the recess bell rang?
6   Explain what happened when the wind blew Katy's bonnet?
7   What did Katy imagine the Miller girls would do to her bonnet?
8   What happened when the little Millerite told the others that Katy was in their playground?
9   What effect did Katy's headlong plunge into her group of friends have upon them?

Sounds

Object	Sound
anvil	clang
bagpipes	skirl
bell	peal; tinkle
bow	twang
brakes	grinding
bullet	ping
chains	jangle; rattle
coins	clink; jingle
corks	pop
dishes	rattle; clatter
engine	throb
explosion	blast
hinges	creak
rifle	report
silk	rustle
siren	wail
skirts	swish
stream	babble; murmur
thunder	clap; peal
wings	whirr

A Write the missing words; some you learnt in Books 2 and 3.

1 the twang of a ____
2 the call of a ____
3 the tinkle of a ____
4 the jingle of ____
5 the shuffle of ____
6 the rustle of ____
7 the grinding of ____
8 the babble of a ____
9 the lash of a ____
10 the skirl of ____
11 the ____ of skirts
12 the ____ of dishes
13 the ____ of corks
14 the ____ of a bullet
15 the ____ of hoofs
16 the ____ of raindrops
17 the ____ of a rifle
18 the ____ of chains
19 the ____ of an anvil
20 a ____ of thunder

B Write in order the words necessary to complete these sentences.

1 With a noisy ____ of wings thousands of starlings descended on the town.

2 The bridal pair left the church to the merry ____ of bells.

3 The workmen were temporarily deafened by the ____ of the explosion.

4 The frequent ____ of the anvil showed how busy the blacksmith was.

5 When hinges ____ they require oiling.

6 The ____ of the siren announced that a fire had broken out.

7 The Highland regiment marched to the ____ of bagpipes.

8 Derek tossed restlessly in his bunk, disturbed by the ____ of the ship's engines.

Analogies

A **young sheep** is called a **lamb**.

A **young cow** is called a **calf**.

So **sheep** is to **lamb** as **cow** is to **calf**.

Or **lamb** is to **sheep** as **calf** is to **cow**.

Such comparisons or likenesses are called analogies.

A   In each line below, consider how the words in the first pair are related, then write the missing word.

1   **Lion** is to **den** as **pig** is to ____ .

2   **Father** is to **son** as **king** is to ____ .

3   **Orange** is to **peel** as **cheese** is to ____ .

4   **Nose** is to **smell** as **eye** is to ____ .

5   **Train** is to **station** as **ship** is to ____ .

6   **Soldier** is to **army** as **sailor** is to ____ .

7   **Teacher** is to **school** as **nurse** is to ____ .

B

1   **Driver** is to **train** as ____ is to **plane**.

2   **Knife** is to **sheath** as ____ is to **scabbard**.

3   **Tailor** is to **clothes** as ____ is to **bread**.

4   **Sheep** is to **flock** as ____ is to **pack**.

5   **Pig** is to **pork** as ____ is to **venison**.

6   **Famine** is to **food** as ____ is to **water**.

7   **Dog** is to **bark** as ____ is to **trumpet**.

C   There is another way of writing these analogies.
sheep : lamb :: cow : calf

1   **bank : manager :: school :**

2   **hand : palm :: foot :**

3   **teacher : pupil :: doctor :**

4   **bird : air :: fish :**

5   **bee : insect :: snake**

6   **husband : wife :: earl :**

7   **house : floor :: ship**

Doers of actions

Action	Doer
apply	applicant
auction	auctioneer
burgle	burglar
capture	captor
challenge	challenger
compete	competitor
contribute	contributor
correspond	correspondent
criticize	critic
dictate	dictator
edit	editor
guard	guardian
lie	liar
mutiny	mutineer
operate	operator
oppose	opponent
preside	president
represent	representative
succeed	successor
survive	survivor

Memorize this list, then answer the questions.

A   What word is used for:

1   one who challenges?
2   one who contributes?
3   one who edits?
4   one who presides?
5   one who lies?
6   one who criticizes?
7   one who applies?
8   one who operates?
9   one who competes?
10   one who survives?

B   Complete each sentence by inserting the word for the doer of the action.

1   A ____ broke into the bank last night.   **burgle**

2   The young orphan was accompanied by his ____ .   **guard**

3   In two hours the ____ had sold all the paintings.   **auction**

4   One ____ was shot in the chest.   **mutiny**

5   The prisoner was treated well by his ____ .   **capture**

6   A ____ of the company called to demonstrate their automatic washing machine.   **represent**

7   Some countries do not have a monarch or a president; they have a ____ .   **dictate**

8   In less than a minute the wrestler had thrown his ____ .   **oppose**

9   The retiring caretaker showed his ____ round the school.   **succeed**

10   The film star ordered a photograph to be sent to every ____ .   **correspond**

Twin words

Learn this list of **twin words** before answering the questions which follow. Exercise B shows how these expressions are used.

bag and baggage
beck and call
body and soul
fame and fortune
fire and water
hale and hearty
hue and cry
neck and neck
rack and ruin
rough and ready
sixes and sevens
spick and span

A Copy these expressions and insert the missing words.

1 fame and ____
2 ____ and ready
3 hale and ____
4 ____ and neck
5 beck and ____
6 ____ and sevens
7 body and ____
8 ____ and ruin
9 fire and ____
10 ____ and span
11 bag and ____
12 ____ and cry

B What are the words omitted from these sentences?

1 Everything at the little hotel was very rough and ____ .

2 For the last fifty metres the two horses were running neck and ____ .

3 The poor widow's pension was barely enough to keep ____ and soul together.

4 The pageboy was at everybody's ____ and call.

5 There was a ____ and cry as the pickpocket fled down the street, followed by a big crowd.

6 The dishonest lodger was put out ____ and baggage.

7 A man will go through ____ and water for the woman he loves.

8 Unfortunately the beautiful old mansion had been allowed to go to rack and ____ .

9 A spick and ____ room is spotlessly clean and very neat and tidy.

10 Many a Briton has decided to seek ____ and fortune in Australia.

82

Rhymes

in
kin
admire
attire
thin
pin
bigger
figure
head
red
skin
chin

A   Write the words, numbered from 1 to 12, which fill the spaces in this extract from a poem.

"Come in," the Mayor cried, looking ____ : 1
And in did come the strangest ____ ! 2
His queer long coat from heel to ____ , 3
Was half of yellow and half of ____ , 4
And he himself was tall and ____ , 5
With sharp blue eyes, each like a ____ , 6
And light loose hair, yet swarthy ____ , 7
No tuft on cheek, nor beard on ____ , 8
But lips where smiles went out and ____ ; 9
There was no guessing his kith and ____   10
And nobody could enough ____   11
The tall man and his quaint ____ . 12

B   Each of these lines contains three rhyming words from which some of the letters are missing. Complete each word.

Example   1   work
                    jerk
                    shirk

1   work   2   home   3   grows
    j _ _ _   f _ _ _   ch _ _ _
    sh _ _ _   c _ _ _   fr _ _ _

4   course   5   become   6   stole
    f _ _ _ _   cr _ _ _   sh _ _ _
    h _ _ _ _ _   gl _ _   scr _ _ _

7   nurse   8   cheer   9   bought
    v _ _ _ _   sm _ _ _   c _ _ _ _ _
    w _ _ _ _   sph _ _ _   t _ _ _

C   Write as eight lines of poetry:

I have a garden of my own, shining with flowers of every hue; I loved it dearly while alone, but I shall love it more with you: and there the golden bees shall come in summer-time at break of morn, and wake us with their busy hum, around the Silea's fragrant thorn.

A fight in a signal-tower

Up over the edge of the spur, three wild horsemen appeared heading for the gateway.

As they dropped from their ponies in the courtyard below, Marcus and Esca drew back from the parapet. "Only three, so far," Marcus whispered. "Don't use your knife unless you have to. They may be of more use to us living than dead."

Esca nodded, and returned his hunting-knife to his belt. Life and the urgency of doing had taken hold of them again. Flattened against the wall on either side of the stairhead they waited, listening to their pursuers questing through storehouse and guardroom. "Fools!" Marcus breathed, as a shout told them that the stairway had been spotted; and then came a rush of feet that checked at the floor below and then came on, storming upward.

Marcus was a good boxer, and much practice with the cestus last winter had made Esca something of a boxer also; together, weary though they were, they made a dangerous team. The first two tribesmen to come ducking out through the low doorway went down without a sound, like poled oxen; the third, not so completely caught unawares, put up more of a fight. Esca flung himself upon him, and they crashed down several steps together, in a flailing mass of arms and legs. There was a short, desperate struggle before Esca came uppermost, and staggering clear, heaved an unconscious man over the doorsill.

The Eagle of the Ninth   Rosemary Sutcliff

1 Where were Marcus and Esca when the horsemen appeared?
2 Where did the horsemen dismount?
3 Which words suggest there might have been more horsemen to come?
4 Why did Marcus advise Esca not to use his knife?
5 Where did Esca keep his knife?
6 Where were their pursuers searching for them?
7 Why did Marcus describe their pursuers as fools?
8 What kind of training had made Esca into a boxer?
9 Why did the third tribesman put up more of a fight than the other two?
10 In what state was the third tribesman after the fight?

Double negatives

Words containing **not** or **no** are called **negatives**.

Examples
no   not   nobody   nothing
nowhere   none   never (*not
ever*)

Two negatives should never be used together in the same sentence.

Wrong
He did **not** tell me **nothing** about it. (*two negatives*)

Right
He did **not** tell me anything about it. (*one negative*)

He told me **nothing** about it. (*one negative*)

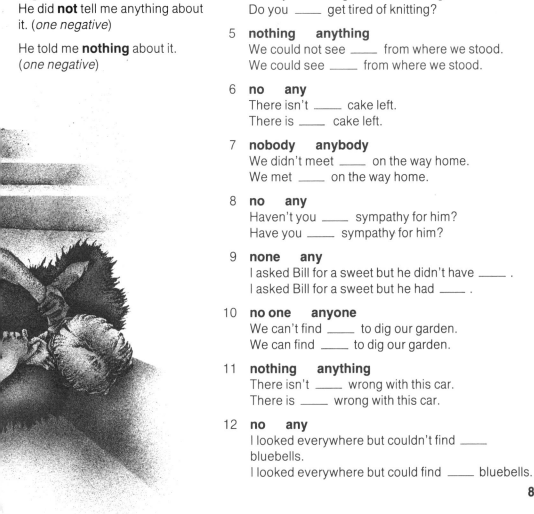

Choose the correct word from the pair above to complete each sentence.

1 **nothing   anything**
John did not tell his father ____ about the accident.
John told his father ____ about the accident.

2 **nowhere   anywhere**
We couldn't find the book ____ .
The book was ____ to be found.

3 **nothing   anything**
The gardener didn't pay Tom ____ for his help.
The gardener paid Tom ____ for his help.

4 **never   ever**
Don't you ____ get tired of knitting?
Do you ____ get tired of knitting?

5 **nothing   anything**
We could not see ____ from where we stood.
We could see ____ from where we stood.

6 **no   any**
There isn't ____ cake left.
There is ____ cake left.

7 **nobody   anybody**
We didn't meet ____ on the way home.
We met ____ on the way home.

8 **no   any**
Haven't you ____ sympathy for him?
Have you ____ sympathy for him?

9 **none   any**
I asked Bill for a sweet but he didn't have ____ .
I asked Bill for a sweet but he had ____ .

10 **no one   anyone**
We can't find ____ to dig our garden.
We can find ____ to dig our garden.

11 **nothing   anything**
There isn't ____ wrong with this car.
There is ____ wrong with this car.

12 **no   any**
I looked everywhere but couldn't find ____ bluebells.
I looked everywhere but could find ____ bluebells.

Proverbs

Learn these proverbs and their meanings well before attempting the questions.

Charity begins at home.	Be kind to relatives before showing kindness to strangers.
What's sauce for the goose is sauce for the gander	One person should be entitled to the same treatment as another.
It is never too late to mend	However old a person is it is not too late for him to reform.
Every cloud has a silver lining	However dark the present may seem the future holds something brighter.
A bird in the hand is worth two in the bush	It is wiser to accept an offer now than to depend on a better offer you may have in the future.

A

1 What has every cloud got?

2 Where does charity begin?

3 What do barking dogs seldom do?

4 What is worth two birds in the bush?

B Complete these proverbs. Give the meanings of Nos. 2, 3, 5, 8 and 9.

1 A friend in need . . .

2 Strike while the . . .

3 Charity begins . . .

4 What's sauce for the goose . . .

5 A bird in the hand . . .

6 Every cloud . . .

7 It is never too late . . .

8 A stitch in time . . .

9 A rolling stone . . .

10 Necessity is the . . .

11 Look before you . . .

Similes

Learn this list of **similes** thoroughly before attempting the exercises.

as blind as a bat
as dry as dust
as frisky as a lamb
as large as life
as pale as death
as sound as a bell
as tender as a chicken
as thick as thieves
as timid as a mouse
as tough as leather

Complete these similes.

A

1 as pale as ____
2 as dry as ____
3 as blind as a ____
4 as thick as ____
5 as frisky as a ____
6 as ____ as a bell
7 as ____ as a chicken
8 as ____ as a mouse
9 as ____ as leather
10 as ____ as life

B   Revision

1 as meek as a ____
2 as pleased as ____
3 as patient as ____
4 as slippery as an ____
5 as smooth as ____
6 as ____ as a new pin
7 as ____ as a button
8 as ____ as brass
9 as ____ as sugar
10 as ____ as a fiddle

C   Write the words which have been omitted from these sentences.

1 The two women in the wrecked car were as pale as ____ .

2 The little girl is as timid as a ____ .

3 One guest at the guest house complained that the beef was as tough as ____ .

4 The new puppy was as frisky as a ____ .

5 The two boys were as thick as ____ .

6 The old gentleman is getting as blind as a ____ .

7 In walked Mr. Micawber, as large as ____ .

8 After being repaired the toy was as sound as a ____ .

9 Sheila found the book as dry as ____ .

10 Alan woke up feeling as ____ as a button.

Fun with words

By rearranging some of the
letters in the word
separate
we can make other words.

Examples   spear
           spare
           pears
           rates
           stare
           steep etc.

A   In the same way, use the letters of the word in
bold type below to form words to complete the
sentences which follow.

consecrated

1   The _ _ _ _ _ Tom threw broke the kitchen window.

2   A church is a very _ _ _ _ _ _ building.

3   When you _ _ _ _ _ at something you look at it with a
fixed gaze.

4   The Fairy Queen was _ _ _ _ _ _ on her throne.

5   A horse is sometimes called a _ _ _ _ _ .

6   A male honey-bee is called a _ _ _ _ _ .

7   A _ _ _ _ _ _ is something you do not wish others to
know.

B   Write the six words in the list below which
cannot be formed from the letters in the word:

comparative

1	private	7	carton	13	compare
2	cramp	8	vicar	14	repair
3	create	9	crêpe	15	taper
4	viper	10	prove	16	voter
5	price	11	carrot	17	treat
6	cream	12	crate	18	impart

C   In each line find the word which corresponds to
one of the given meanings. By rearranging the
letters of this word you have the word which
matches the other meaning.

1   the staff of life;
hair on the face

2   the backbone;
evergreen trees with needle-shaped leaves

3   a room where butter is made;
a record of daily happenings

4   another word for "wept";
a drink made from the juice of apples

Idioms

Learn this list of idioms and their meanings, then work the test which follows.

Idiom	Meaning
to send to Coventry	to ignore a person
to play second fiddle	to take a back place while someone else leads
to take French leave	to go off without permission
to be at loggerheads	to be quarrelling
to make a mountain out of a molehill	to make trifling difficulties appear great ones
to feather one's nest	to increase one's possessions
to pay through the nose	to pay too high a price
to smell a rat	to be suspicious
to give a person the cold shoulder	to make him feel unwelcome
to blow one's own trumpet	to boast about oneself

Rewrite these sentences substituting for the words in bold type one of the **idioms** in the list.

1 Robinson paid **far too high a price** for his house.

2 It is wrong to think only of **adding to one's possessions**.

3 Some people prefer **to take a back place and let someone else take the lead**.

4 Very soon the police began **to be suspicious**.

5 Alan is too fond of **boasting about himself**.

6 The two neighbours are forever **quarrelling**.

7 Faint-hearted people often like making **difficulties appear much greater than they really are**.

8 The blackleg's mates **ignored him and refused to talk to him**.

9 The soldier took **the week-end off without the permission of his commanding officer**.

10 The old couple decided to give the tramp **the impression that he was most unwelcome**.

Long John Silver

Long John Silver, our ship's cook – Barbecue, as the men called him – carried his crutch by a lanyard round his neck, to have both hands as free as possible. It was something to see him wedge the foot of his crutch against a bulkhead, and, propped against it, yielding to every movement of the ship, get on with his cooking like someone safe ashore. Still more strange was it to see him in the heaviest of weather cross the deck. He had a line or two rigged up to help him across the widest spaces, and he would hand himself from one place to another, as quickly as another man could walk.

"He's no common man, Barbecue," said the coxswain to me. "He had good schooling in his young days, and can speak like a book when so minded, and he's brave – a lion's nothing alongside of Long John! I've seen him grapple four men, and knock their heads together – and him unarmed."

All the crew respected and even obeyed him. He had a way of doing everybody some particular service. To me he was unweariedly kind; and always glad to see me in the galley.

"Hawkins," he would say, "come and have a yarn with John. Nobody more welcome than yourself, my son. Here's Cap'n Flint – I calls my parrot Cap'n Flint after the famous buccaneer – here's Cap'n Flint predicting success to our voyage. Wasn't you, cap'n?"

And the parrot would say, with great rapidity, "Pieces of eight! pieces of eight! pieces of eight!" till you wondered that it was not out of breath, or till John threw his handkerchief over the cage.

Treasure Island   Robert Louis Stevenson

1 What nickname did the crew give Long John Silver?
2 How did John carry his crutch?
3 Why did he carry it in this way?
4 How did he use his crutch when cooking?
5 What helped John to cross the widest spaces of the deck in the heaviest weather?
6 What example of John's bravery did the coxswain give?
7 Why did the crew respect John?
8 What was the name of John's parrot?
9 After whom was he named?
10 How did John stop the parrot talking?

ANSWERS

Page 1 Nouns

A

milkfloat	milk-bottles	chimneys
tyres	crates	windows
wheels	milkman	door
steering-wheel	cap	gate
windscreen	shirt	woman
windscreen-wiper	tie	fence
lights	trousers	trees
nameboard	jacket	shrubs
lettering	shoes	path
driving-seat	cat	clouds
milk	house	birds
	roof	

B

1. car; ice; tree
2. diamonds; rubies; emeralds; stones
3. players; team
4. dog; man; friend
5. city; country; capital
6. heart; blood; body
7. rust; oxygen; air
8. referee; player; field

C

1. restaurant
2. helicopter
3. palette
4. triangle
5. dollar

Page 2 Verbs

A

1. breathe
4. digging; raked
2. hibernate
5. produces; exports
3. wake; search
6. struck; sank

B

apologize	to express regret	fortify	to make strong
bewilder	to confuse completely	glare	to stare in anger
comprehend	to understand	hibernate	to spend the winter asleep
confess	to own up to a sin	inhale	to breathe in
confide	to tell as a secret	loathe	to regard with disgust
demolish	to pull or tear down	meditate	to think quietly
devour	to eat like an animal	pester	to annoy; to irritate
discuss	to talk over	relax	to become less stiff or firm
expose	to uncover; to lay open	strive	to work hard or try hard
extinguish	to put out; to wipe out	unite	to join together

Page 3 Adjectives

A

1. tame; affectionate
4. Tame; sociable; quarrelsome
2. sound; ripe; dry; clean
5. short; webbed; thick
3. Canadian; vast; huge
6. rough; interlocking

B

arrogant	boastfully proud	memorable	not to be forgotten
boisterous	very noisy and disorderly	obstinate	stubborn
contemptuous	very scornful	pompous	self-important
distinguished	well-known; famous	ponderous	heavy and clumsy
elaborate	worked out with great care	prosperous	successful; thriving
frantic	wild with rage or pain	radiant	bright; shining
gorgeous	richly coloured; splendid	repulsive	causing strong dislike
hospitable	giving a warm welcome	stagnant	not running or flowing
intelligent	quick at learning	stationary	not moving
laborious	requiring much work	tumultuous	rough; violent

Page 4   Adverbs

A
1 carefully *how*
2 frequently *when*
3 away *where*
4 aimlessly *how*
5 shortly *when*
6 noisily *how*

B
1 violently
2 patiently
3 merrily
4 bitterly
5 awkwardly
6 courageously
7 frugally
8 hungrily
9 contentedly
10 politely
11 mournfully
12 uproariously
13 gracefully
14 soundly
15 distinctly
16 intimately

Page 5   Nouns—number

A
1 pianos
2 sheaves
3 chimneys
4 heroes
5 mice
6 diaries
7 geese
8 photos
9 thieves
10 chiefs
11 deer
12 Eskimos
13 factories
14 sons-in-law
15 men

B
1 factories
2 turkeys
3 chiefs
4 potatoes
5 thieves
6 wolves
7 pianos
8 deer
9 oxen
10 mice

C
1 The thieves removed the turkeys from the shelves.
2 The Eskimos were armed with long knives.
3 The heroes had their photos taken.
4 The children looked at the little white mice.
5 The foxes looked longingly at the geese.

Page 6   Attacked by a crow

1. Silver was almost at the crest of the slope.
2. Pipkin was screaming because he was being attacked by the crow.
3. The crow had chosen Pipkin and Fiver for attack because they were so small and tired.
4. The crow aimed at Fiver with its great bill.
5. Pipkin buried his head in a clump of rank grass.
6. Hazel ran to Pipkin's aid.
7. He succeeded in distracting the crow's attention.
8. He compares it to the sound of a snail-shell when a thrush beats it on a stone.
9. Silver and the crow stood face to face.
10. Bigwig ran straight into the crow from behind and knocked it sideways.

Page 7   Alphabetical order

A
building
bus
fire-engine
helicopter
jet
motor-bike

B

1	2	3
shudder	passport	capsule
signal	peculiar	chorus
skier	physical	climate
society	plumber	crusade
student	portable	curfew

C

1	2	3
bladder	granite	sparrow
bleak	grease	spectre
blizzard	gristle	spiral
blockade	ground	splint
blunder	gruesome	sprawl

D

1	2	3
catalogue	problem	spray
catch	proceed	spread
catgut	produce	sprint
catkin	profit	sprout
cattle	promise	spruce

4	retail	5	patch
	retire		patent
	retort		patient
	retreat		patriot
	return		pattern

Page 8 Verbs—past tense and participle

A
1	fought	2	fled	3	slew
4	laid	5	hurt	6	wove

Page 9 Verbs past tense and participle (contd.)

7	mistook	8	drowned

B
1 gone
2 thought
3 hurt
4 chosen
5 woven
6 hanged
7 shown
8 frozen

C
1 bore
2 broken
3 blown
4 begun
5 drove
6 beaten
7 lay
8 wrung

Page 10 Sentences and phrases

A
1	sentence	2	phrase	3	phrase
4	sentence	5	sentence	6	phrase
7	phrase	8	sentence		

B
Own answers.

Page 11 Nouns—gender

A
1	madam	2	spinster	3	lady
4	mayoress	5	peahen	6	empress
7	marchioness	8	cow	9	niece
0	heiress				

B

1 drake
4 wizard
7 nephew
10 emperor

2 boar
5 stag
8 ram

3 widower
6 host
9 buck

C

1 proprietress
4 niece

2 peahen
5 marchioness

3 conductress
6 Madam

D

1 sows
4 Lady

2 duck
5 ewe

3 bull
6 hind

Page 12   Toad and company

1 Toad set his companions to capture the old grey horse.
2 He took a good deal of catching because he preferred the paddock.
3 Toad hung nose-bags, nets of onions, bundles of hay and baskets from the bottom of the cart.
4 The animals were sitting on the shaft.
5 The birds called and whistled cheerily to the travellers.
6 The wayfarers said 'Good day' when they passed the travellers.
7 These people said nice things about their beautiful cart.
8 Toad and Company drew up on a remote common far from habitations.
9 They turned the horse loose to graze.
10 They ate their supper sitting on the grass.

Page 13   Nouns—formation

A

1 imagination
2 advice
3 explosion
4 destruction
5 conversation
6 advertisement
7 applause
8 pronunciation
9 accusation
10 complaint

B

1 choice
2 abolition
3 decision
4 explanation
5 satisfaction
6 pursuit
7 inquiry
8 completion
9 deceit
10 acquaintance

Page 14 Adjectives—formation

A
1 fluffy
2 squeaky
3 starchy
4 wealthy
5 frosty

B
1 stony
2 wavy
3 greasy
4 breezy
5 tasty
6 pebbly

C
1 furry
2 tinny
3 knotty
4 boggy
5 witty
6 skinny

Page 15 Direct speech

A
1 "Your shoelace is undone, Barbara," said Wendy.
2 "Did you remember to bring a loaf, Sonia?" asked her mother.
3 "These cauliflowers were cut this morning, madam," said the greengrocer.
4 "Keep him in bed for a few days," advised the doctor.

B
1 The dentist said, "You should have that tooth filled."
2 Linda remarked, "This is the tastiest meal I have had for a long time."
3 Handing him ten pence the old lady said, "Thank you for your help, my boy."
4 The auctioneer asked, "Is there any advance on fifty pounds?"

C
1 "Please sir," said Oliver Twist to the master, "I want some more."
2 "Oh dear," sighed the old lady, "I have lost the key of the house."
3 "You will have to hurry, Mary," exclaimed her mother, "or you will be late for school!"
4 "Stand to attention," shouted the sergeant, "and hold your heads up."

Page 16 Other words for said and asked

A
1 .... remarked the boatman
2 .... whispered her mother
3 .... urged his teacher
4 .... shouted the skipper
5 .... stammered the frightened boy
6 .... admitted Carol
7 .... boasted Alan
8 .... announced the headmaster

B
1 .... ordered the surgeon
2 .... inquired the stranger
3 .... replied the policeman
4 .... coaxed Elizabeth
5 .... protested the customer
6 .... prophesied Aunt Jane
7 .... complained the farmer
8 .... grumbled the shop assistant

Page 17   Collective nouns

A		B		C	
1	choir	1	angels	1	band
2	staff	2	trees	2	plague; swarm
3	brood	3	stars	3	brood
4	peal	4	pilgrims	4	clump
5	company	5	directors	5	company
6	swarm; plague	6	minstrels	6	gang
7	crowd	7	arrows	7	board
8	gang	8	magistrates	8	crowd
9	pride	9	worshippers	9	host
10	flight	10	eggs	10	flight

Page 18   Wildlife in danger

1   Some species of wild animal may become extinct because streams and rivers have become polluted and because pesticides intended for killing insects that are pests also destroy many that are not. (An increase in building has disturbed and destroyed much of the countryside that provides homes for wild animals. Many species of wild animal are hunted and killed by man for pleasure or for profit.)
2   It has become common practice because industry has grown enormously.
3   Insects classified as pests are intended to be destroyed by pesticides.
4   An increase in population has meant an increase in building which has brought about the destruction of much of the countryside.
5   It is under threat because it is hunted by sportsmen.
6   Borneo and Sumatra have smuggling problems.
7   The chinchilla is hunted for its fur.
8   Whales are hunted for the oil and food they yield.
9   Sewage pollution has been greatly reduced.
10 A ban on trading in some furs has been agreed. (Organisations like Friends of the Earth have been formed and do valuable work.)

Page 19   Fun with words

A

1	a	harp	2	a	monk	3	a	kid
	b	harpoon		b	monkey		b	kidnap
4	a	hat	5	a	cent	6	a	port
	b	hatchet		b	centre		b	portion
7	a	halt	8	a	host	9	a	boy
	b	halter		b	hostile		b	boycott
10	a	mass						
	b	massacre						

B

1	S C A M P	2	C O M E S	3	P A N I C
4	S N I P E	5	S P A C E	6	5 4 7 1 8
7	2 7 1 6 8	8	8 7 3 5 1	9	7 3 4 6 2
0	8 5 2 6 1				

Page 20   Using the right adjective

A

a   b

1 frantic   struggles
2 antique   furniture
3 affectionate   daughter
4 formidable   task
5 palatable   meal
6 injurious   drugs
7 threadbare   clothes
8 meagre   allowance
9 precipitous   slope
0 relentless   grip

B

1   vivid
2   luscious
3   prosperous
4   shrewd
5   sumptuous
6   riotous
7   abundant
8   candid
9   secluded
10 righteous

Page 21   Pronouns

A

1 she; her
2 he; it
3 We
4 us
5 them
6 they
7 his

B

1 yourselves
2 yourself
3 itself
4 myself
5 herself
6 ourselves

Page 22   Homophones

A

1 cereal
2 currant
3 foul
4 heir
5 brake

B

1 cheque; check
2 boy; buoy
3 aloud; allowed
4 course; coarse
5 beach; beech

Page 23   Abbreviations

A

1 Member of Parliament
2 Department
3 National Society for the Prevention of Cruelty to Children
4 care of
5 Her Royal Highness
6 Royal Society for the Prevention of Cruelty to Animals
7 postcard
8 Justice of the Peace

B

1 Telephone
2 On Her Majesty's Service
3 Royal Navy (Naval)
4 Automobile Association
5 United Nations
6 Doctor of Medicine
7 Medical Officer of Health

Page 24   Rikki-tikki and Darzee

1 He licked his lips because he had found a splendid hunting-ground.
2 His tail grew more bushy and bristly at the thought of it.
3 Rikki heard very sorrowful voices in a thornbush.
4 They make a nest by pulling two big leaves together, stitching them up the edges with fibres and filling the hollow with cotton and downy fluff.
5 They were crying because one of their babies had fallen out of the nest and Nag had eaten him.
6 The low hiss came from the thick grass at the foot of the bush.
7 They cowered down in the nest.
8 It made him jump back two clear feet.
9 Nag was five feet long from tongue to tail.

Page 25   Letter writing

Own answers.

Page 26 Occupations

A
1. waitress
2. steeplejack
3. cricketer
4. announcer
5. librarian
6. nurse
7. butcher
8. plumber

B
1. librarian
2. tobacconist
3. waitress
4. chemist
5. jeweller
6. florist
7. butcher
8. steeplejack
9. postwoman
10. nurse

Page 27 Group names

A
1. vehicles
2. vegetables
3. tools
4. cutlery
5. crockery
6. footwear

B
1. venison; names of meats
2. synagogue; places of worship
3. alligator; names of reptiles
4. villa; kinds of dwellings
5. silver; names of metals
6. baker; kinds of traders

C

Weapons	Vessels	Furniture	Footwear
rifle	liner	cupboard	clogs
dagger	trawler	table	sandals
spear	submarine	armchair	shoes
sword	schooner	sideboard	boots
pistol	yacht	wardrobe	slippers
revolver	cruiser	cabinet	wellingtons

Page 28 Comparing adjectives

A

	Positive degree	Comparative degree	Superlative degree
1	lovely	lovelier	loveliest
2	large	larger	largest
3	hot	hotter	hottest
4	noisy	noisier	noisiest
5	slim	slimmer	slimmest
6	wise	wiser	wisest
7	wet	wetter	wettest
8	wealthy	wealthier	wealthiest
9	fine	finer	finest
0	greedy	greedier	greediest

B
1 more capable 2 most intelligent 3 more generous

Page 29 Comparing adjectives (contd.)

B		C	
4	most expensive	1	worst
5	more dangerous	2	worse
6	most wonderful	3	better
7	most important	4	worse
8	more interesting	5	best
		6	most
		7	smallest
		8	less

Page 30 The score card

1 A. Booth was the highest scorer.
2 His score was 17 short of a century.
3 Two batsmen were clean bowled – R. Dale and D. Macmillan.
4 D. Macmillan was bowled for a "duck".
5 Gibson made a catch off his own bowling.
6 T. E. Dexter was undefeated at the end of the innings.
7 L. Jones was caught before he had scored.
7 B. R. Lock was out leg before wicket.
9 The name of Royford's wicket-keeper was Jagger.
10 He played well, stumping two and catching two.
11 Moss performed the "hat trick".
12 Royford need to make 266 for a first innings lead.

Page 31 Conjunctions

A
1 The boy got out of bed and stretched his arms.
2 We intended to swim but the water was too cold.
3 The cinema was full so we went back home.
4 The children made their way home for (as, because) it was getting dark.
5 Ben made some tea while his mother bathed the baby.
6 The wind was icy cold for it was still winter.
7 She was very unpopular because she was so sarcastic.
8 You can do it yourself since you are so clever.

B

1 or
4 although
7 until (unless)

2 unless
5 whether (if)
8 where

3 after (although)
6 if

Page 32 Opposites—using a prefix

A

1 insane
4 unusual
7 inequality
10 imperfect
13 discontinue

2 unaware
5 disobedient
8 dissimilar
11 ingratitude
14 inconsiderate

3 inhuman
6 disapprove
9 uncertain
12 disregard
15 disorderly,

B

1 improbable
4 illegal
7 unfortunate

2 immovable
5 irresponsible
8 discourteous

3 ungrateful
6 unnecessary

C

1 an **unpopular** man
2 **irregular** attendance
3 an **inefficient** worker

4 an **unimportant** town
5 **unfavourable** weather
6 an **improper** remark

Page 33 People

A

1 hypocrite
2 traitor
3 tyrant
4 lunatic
5 exile

B

1 prophet
2 pedestrian
3 genius
4 vandal
5 mimic

Page 34 Proper adjectives

A

1 Spanish
4 Chinese
7 Maltese
10 Swedish

2 Greek
5 Dutch
8 Norwegian

3 Danish
6 Israeli
9 Alpine

B

1 Belgian
4 Swiss
7 Icelandic

2 Mexican
5 Turkish
8 Venetian

3 Polish
6 Portuguese

Page 35   Nouns—possession

A

1 Ann's dress
2 the knight's sword
3 the tailor's thimble
4 the butcher's block
5 the cricketer's pads
6 the lion's jaws
7 the winner's reward
8 the boxer's gloves
9 the comedian's jokes

B

1 the miners' lamps
2 the elephants' tusks
3 the sailors' quarters
4 the porters' room
5 the girls' playground
6 the monkeys' tails
7 the insects' wings
8 the birds' nests
9 the ladies' cloakroom

C

1 a woman's handbag
2 the oxen's yokes
3 the mice's tails
4 the policemen's helmets
5 the children's toys
6 the men's shoes
7 the airmen's camp
8 the frogmen's feet
9 the geese's honks

Page 36   Sea-lions

1 A sea-lion is bigger.
2 A fully grown sea-lion is from twelve to twenty feet long.
3 A sea-lion's skin is about an inch in thickness.
4 At least a foot of fat lies between the skin and its flesh or bones.
5 The tail and fins serve the sea-lion for feet.
6 The sea-lion is at sea all the summer.
7 It is on shore all the winter.
8 Young sea-lions are born in the winter.
9 The male has a large trunk or snout, hanging down five or six inches which the female has not.
10 The males fight chiefly about their females.

Page 37   Contractions

A

1 they'd
4 he'd
2 we'd
5 she'd
3 you'd
6 I'd

B

1 I'm
4 won't
7 they're
10 it's
13 I'd
16 you're
19 can't
2 you've
5 he'd
8 shan't
11 haven't
14 we're
17 we'd
20 they'll
3 she's
6 don't
9 we've
12 she'll
15 aren't
18 they've

C

1 cannot; I am
4 We have; We will
2 we are
3 you are

Page 38   Antonyms—opposites

A
1 sorrow	2 spendthrift	3 expensive
4 deny	5 forbid	6 knowledge
7 innocent	8 retreat	9 solid
10 departure	11 timid	12 humble
13 true	14 scarce	15 success
16 wealth	17 loiter	18 reveal

B
1 expensive	2 absent	3 false
4 spendthrift	5 loiters	6 Ignorance

C
1 guilty	2 plentiful	3 forbid
innocent	scarce	permit
4 timid	5 poverty	
bold	wealth	

Page 39   Direct and indirect speech

A
1 Philip asked his mother if he might have another plum.
2 Mr. Dean said that he had a bad headache and that he thought he would lie down.
3 Mr. Caldwell remarked that the days were certainly getting longer.
4 David asked Roger if he knew how to play darts.
5 Mrs. Smith told her son that he looked as if he could do with a good holiday.
6 Peter's father told him to wash his hands before coming to the table.
7 The old lady invited Mrs. Dale to go inside and have tea with them.

B
1 "Your shoes will be ready by Saturday," the shoe repairer told Robert.
2 "Have you loitered on the way home from school, Simon?" asked his mother.
3 "Have you ever spent a holiday in France, Bernard?" asked his teacher.
4 "I once spent a month in a villa on the Riviera," replied Bernard.
5 "Your work is improving," the headmaster told the boys.
6 "I have come top in English," Judith told her father.
7 "I'm delighted to see you getting on so well!" exclaimed her father, and gave her forty pence.

Page 40   Compound words

A
sea+weed = seaweed	light+house = lighthouse	star+fish = starfish
sand+castle = sandcastle	speed+boat = speedboat	break+water = breakwater
sea+shell = seashell	life+belt = lifebelt	sea+boots = seaboots
fisher+man = fisherman	life+boat = lifeboat	sea+shore = seashore

B

1	woodpecker	1	sawdust	1	buttonhole
2	postbox	2	waistcoat	2	silkworm
3	penknife	3	passport	3	molehill
4	skyscraper	4	speedboat	4	sandpaper
5	pickpocket	5	foxglove	5	footlights
6	breakwater	6	windscreen		
7	honeycomb	7	shipwreck		
8	rattlesnake	8	mantelpiece		
9	buttercup	9	millwheel		
10	threadbare	10	whirlwind		

C (column 3 heading)

Page 41   Diminutives

A

1	elver	10	codling
2	gosling	11	tadpole
3	calf	12	fawn
4	lamb	13	calf
5	leveret	14	rivulet
6	streamlet	15	filly
7	owlet	16	cub
8	foal	17	eaglet
9	puppy	18	cygnet

B

1	elvers
2	filly (foal)
3	hare
4	horse (mare)
5	sheep
6	piglets
7	cygnets
8	kittens

Page 42   The Royal Mint

1 Bristol, Canterbury, London (Winchester; York)
2 It was on Tower Hill, London.
3 It was established at Llantrisant, South Wales.
4 Britain's decimal currency was introduced on 15th February, 1971.
5 The metal ingots are melted in closed crucibles for about two hours and the molten metal is then run into moulds to form coinage-bars.
6 They are passed between rollers to ensure that they are of uniform size.
7 They are fed into annealing drums to soften the metal in preparation for the stamping process.
8 They are counted by an automatic machine.
9 Cupro-nickel is used in place of silver.
10 There would be two thousand 5p pieces.

Page 43   Using the right pronoun

1	I	2	me	3	I
4	me	5	me	6	I
7	me	8	I	9	I
10	me				

Page 44   Fun with words

A

1	loose	2	fable	3	trick
4	clash	5	graft		

B

1	crust	2	shrink	3	harm
4	torn	5	boat		

C

1	farm	2	switch	3	strips
4	boast	5	bond		

D

1	thread	2	clover	3	smite
4	gnash	5	voice		

Page 45   Adjectives—formation

A

1	porous	2	famous	3	envious
4	vigorous	5	spacious	6	prosperous
7	poisonous	8	perilous	9	villainous
10	gluttonous				

B

1	humorous	2	marvellous	3	luxurious
4	glorious	5	furious	6	mischievous
7	riotous	8	continuous	9	injurious
10	miraculous				

Page 46   Proverbs

A

1	saves nine	2	honesty	3	necessity
4	moss				

B

1 A rolling stone gathers no moss.
2 Cut your coat according to your cloth.
3 A friend in need is a friend indeed.

4   Fine feathers make fine birds.
5   Honesty is the best policy.
6   Strike while the iron is hot.
7   A stitch in time saves nine.
8   Necessity is the mother of invention.
9   Birds of a feather flock together.
10 Too many cooks spoil the broth.

C

1 iron   2 need   3 stitch

Page 47   Similes

A		B Book 3		C	
1	button	1	daisy	1	deaf
2	new pin	2	fox	2	bold
3	doorpost	3	pancake	3	dead
4	doornail	4	peacock	4	clean
5	lion	5	lightning	5	bee
6	bold	6	safe	6	cucumber
7	fit	7	light	7	fiddle
8	cool	8	old	8	button
9	sweet	9	poor		
10	busy	10	firm		

Page 48   Inside the vault

1   The small room was very dark because it was underground.
2   The boxes were coffins.
3   Thomas Kempe's box was by itself on the opposite side of the room to where all the other boxes were stacked.
4   31st October.
5   He died in the 17th century.
6   He was 62 years old.
7   He was an apothecary.
8   He was a sorcerer.
9   His true occupation could not be shown because the Church would not have allowed a sorcerer to be buried in the vault.
10 He believed in magic; and he hated priests.

Page 49   Joining sentences

A

1   The police arrested the youth who had robbed the bank.

2 Mrs. Baird gave Angela a bracelet which was made of gold.
3 The door was opened by a girl to whom I handed a letter.
4 This is the house that Jack built.
5 Sitting near us was a woman whose hair had been dyed blue.

B
1 The day was cold and windy for it was only the first day of February.
2 The dog was barking and trying to get over the gate so the children kept away from him.
3 The office had closed and the staff had departed although it was not yet five o'clock.
4 I had intended to go for a walk, but it started to snow so I sat by the fire and fell fast asleep.
5 Andrew had a bad leg and was unable to walk, so he stayed indoors with Gillian who read several stories to him.
6 We set off for the woods, but after a while there was a thunderstorm so we sheltered in an old barn which was close at hand.

Page 50   Abbreviations

A
1 British Summer Time
2 I owe you
3 knock-out
4 by way of
5 miles per gallon
6 per annum (yearly; annually)
7 versus (against)
8 Criminal Investigation Department

B
1 Greenwich Mean Time
2 for example
3 Reply if you please
4 that is
5 note well
6 Tuberculosis
7 Queen's Counsel
8 namely

Page 51   Using the right verb

A
1 reveal
2 inflict
3 evade
4 impart
5 surmount
6 liberate
7 denounce
8 estimate
9 contract
10 trespass
11 foreign language
12 fortune
13 mob
14 request
15 future
16 promise
17 pests
18 catastrophe
19 statement
20 fine

B
1 inherit
2 imposed
3 disperse
4 contracted
5 impart
6 exterminate
7 evaded
8 estimated

Page 52   Idioms

A

	Idiom	Meaning
1	to be under a cloud	to be under suspicion
2	to flog a dead horse	to do work which produces no result
3	to be a dog in a manger	to deny to others what is useless to oneself
4	to draw the long bow	to exaggerate
5	to bury the hatchet	to settle a quarrel and live in peace
6	to have an axe to grind	to have something to gain by an action
7	to take the bull by the horns	to meet difficulties boldly
8	to be a wet blanket	to be a spoilsport
9	to make a clean breast of it	to confess to some wrong
10	to show the white feather	to show cowardice

B

1 The detective determined to take the bull by the horns.
2 Harold told his uncle not to be a wet blanket.
3 The old rivals will soon bury the hatchet.
4 The prefect was under a cloud at school.
5 The old sailor is very fond of drawing the long bow.

Page 53   Synonyms—similars

A

1 forbidden
2 smell
3 short
4 room
5 unbeatable
6 unwilling
7 try
8 scatter
9 height
10 sudden

B

1 famous
2 drunk
3 understand
4 hate
5 show
6 inside
7 friendly
8 sad
9 pierce
10 small

Page 54   A pony for Jody

1 He was caught by complete surprise when he saw the pony.
2 tense; disobedience
3 He was choked with emotion.
4 He warned him that he must feed the pony and clean his stall.
5 Jody was overcome by the sight of the pony and the thought that it might be for him.
6 Jody spoke of the pony with pride because he knew that the pony was going to be his.
7 They were relieved because Jody's words showed that he was pleased with the pony and this broke the tension of the situation.
8 Carl Tiffin wanted to be by himself because he was embarrassed.
9 He could not be ridden for some time because he was just a colt.
10 Billy Buck was going to help Jody break in the pony.

Page 55 Occupations

A

1 mechanic
2 sculptor
3 dentist
4 reporter
5 florist
6 architect
7 fishmonger
8 auctioneer

B

1 solicitor
2 reporter
3 architect
4 detective
5 florist
6 fishmonger
7 auctioneer
8 sculptor
9 mechanic

C

1 caddie
2 florist
3 author
4 chauffeur
5 dentist

Page 56 Sentence structure

A

1 Although she had been warned not to do so Julia persisted in talking.
2 Without thinking how she could pay for it she ordered the dress.
3 On the quay two sailors were having an argument.
4 Just as night was falling the convict was recaptured.
5 With a shriek of its whistle the express train rushed into the tunnel.
6 If you do not check that cough you will be seriously ill.
7 In the great hall of the castle a huge log fire blazed.
8 Long before daybreak the girl was up and about.

B

1 A Christmas Carol was written by Charles Dickens.
2 The Wanderers were beaten by the Rovers 2–0 last Saturday.
3 The valuable portrait was stolen by a gang of thieves.
4 The plans of the dining-hall were drawn by the County Architect.
5 The frail old gentleman was shaken by the heavy fall.
6 Spot was taken to the park by the twins.
7 The curtain was torn by our puppy.
8 The curtains for the lounge were chosen by the three girls.

Page 57 Alphabetical order

A

1 straight
strand
strap
straw
stray

4 forth
fortify
fortnight
fortress
fortunate

2 handful
handicap
handle
handsome
handy

5 partake
partial
party
partner
party

3 catacomb
catalogue
catapult
cataract
catastrophe

6 compare
compel
compile
complain
compose

1	7	2	4	3	7	4	6
5	2	6	2	7	10	8	1
9	8	10	5	11	6	12	5
13	10	14	6	15	4	16	3
17	8	18	7	19	9	20	3

Page 58   Adjectives—formation

A

1	muscular	2	effective	3	fraudulent
4	athletic	5	sympathetic	6	energetic
7	skilful	8	beneficial	9	systematic
10	creditable	11	methodical	12	gigantic
13	scientific	14	fiery	15	picturesque
16	influential	17	circular	18	metallic

B

1	effective	2	skilful	3	metallic
4	athletic	5	scientific	6	circular
7	energetic	8	beneficial	9	nonsensical
10	sympathetic	11	picturesque	12	fraudulent

C

1	systematic	2	methodical	3	creditable
4	customary	5	picturesque		

Page 59   Capital letters

A

1 The River Thames is sometimes referred to as Old Father Thames.
2 Both German and Italian are taught at Grosvenor Grammar School.
3 Rudyard Kipling, who was born in India, wrote many fine books, the most famous being The Jungle Books.
4 Easter is a movable festival which may come in March or April, but Christmas is not.
5 The Bank of England is sometimes called The Old Lady of Threadneedle Street.
6 Linda's brother Colin is a patient at the Middlesex Hospital.
7 The White Tower in the Tower of London was built by Gundulf, Bishop of Rochester, about A.D. 1078.
8 From Monday to Friday the shop closes at 5.30; on Saturdays it closes at 1 o'clock.

B

1 Would you like to tour Europe and see its wonderful sights?
2 In the market there were ample supplies of apples, pears, oranges, bananas, peaches and grapes.
3 "James, did you give my message to the headmaster?" asked his mother.

4 "Yes, Mother, I gave it to him before lessons began," replied James.
5 Some members won't be present but it doesn't matter.
6 The ticket bore the date Thurs. 26th Sept. in bold type.
7 The bat we played with was Tom's but the ball was Duncan's.
8 "Oh, dear," exclaimed Miss Taylor in alarm, "I have lost my purse!"

Page 60 Encounter with a dinosaur

1 It was a cold, misty night.
2 The sound of the fog horn could be heard.
3 There was little visibility as the two men couldn't see far and they couldn't see plainly.
4 A ripple first told the men that there was something in the sea.
5 They saw the ripple far out at sea.
6 It rose a full forty feet.
7 The writer compares the monster's body to a little island of black coral and shells and crayfish.
8 It was ninety or a hundred feet long.
9 He suggested ten million years ago.
10 The monster was not continuously visible because its shape was sometimes blotted out by the fog coming and going about it.

Page 61 Homophones

A
1 veil
2 stationary
3 prophet
4 sow
5 muscle

B
1 herd; heard
2 key; quay
3 knight; night
4 stile; style
5 plaice; place

Page 62 Twin words

A
1	thin	2	touch	3	then
4	wear	5	blood	6	ways
7	short	8	tooth	9	soul
10	well	11	downs	12	short

B
1	means	2	tear	3	go
4	there	5	ups	6	thick
7	flesh	8	good	9	nail
10	soul				

Page 63   Rhymes

A

1	I	2	tower	3	devour
4	rye	5	flour	6	farms
7	see	8	be	9	arms
10	me	11	flails	12	floors
13	doors	14	sails	15	roars

B

1	decline	2	celebrate	3	survey
4	snare	5	campaign	6	interfere
7	receipt	8	Antique	9	rehearse
10	picturesque				

Page 64   Prepositions

A

1	from	2	along	3	before
4	against	5	after	6	around
7	through	8	outside	9	on
10	off				

Page 65   Prepositions (contd.)

B

1	in	2	into	3	to
4	with	5	between	6	among
7	in	8	at	9	beside
10	besides				

C

Own answers.

Page 66   Tarka fights Deadlock

1   Boulders; rocks; seaweed.
2   The animals were invading their territory.
3   They were watching the huntsmen wading into the water.
4   People thought that Tarka had become exhausted and was now floating in the shallow water.
5   He shook his head because he could see no sign of the otter.
6   He prepared to sound his horn to call off the hunt.
7   Tarka's head appeared above the surface of the water.
8   Deadlock's struggle was in vain because Tarka's grip upon him was so tight.
9   Deadlock's hindlegs were above the surface of the water.
10   Tarka loosened his bite because he needed to breathe.

Page 67 Containers

A

barrel   dustbin   rucksack
wallet   chest   cupboard
vase   crate

B

1 chest   2 crate   3 caddy
4 cupboard   5 wardrobe   6 holster
7 quiver   8 rucksack   9 manager
10 barrel

Page 68 Words with more than one meaning

A

1 litter   2 chest   3 charge
4 express   5 ground   6 spring
7 stern   8 plane   9 temple
10 coach

B

Own answers.

Page 69 Occupations

A

1 actress
2 physiotherapist
3 pilot
4 artist
5 surgeon
6 ballerina
7 photographer
8 teacher

B

1 taxidermist
2 interpreter
3 artist
4 beautician
5 pilot
6 engineers
7 solicitor
8 messenger
9 physiotherapist
10 surgeon

Page 70 Antonyms—opposites

A

1 contract   2 defeat   3 minimum
4 glut   5 fine   6 decrease
7 reward   8 minority   9 freedom
10 superior   11 exit   12 opaque
13 reckless   14 ascend   15 export
16 temporary   17 interior   18 voluntary

B

1	entrance	2	coarse	3	victory
4	compulsory	5	ancient	6	exterior
7	attack	8	reckless	9	captivity
10	punishment				

Page 71   People

A
1 wiseacre
2 scapegoat
3 eavesdropper
4 optimist
5 imposter

B
1 pessimist
2 stowaway
3 emigrant
4 vegetarian
5 eavesdropper

Page 72   Gerard and the bear

1 The branch was forty feet above the ground.
2 Denys was standing beneath the tree.
3 The "twang" was caused by Denys's crossbow as he shot his arrows.
4 The bear snarled.
5 Hot blood spurted from her jaws.
6 paralysed
7 It stuck its claws deep into the wood.
8 It shook Gerard forward on his stomach with his face upon one of the bear's paws.
9 Denys cried in dismay because Gerard had fainted and had rolled headlong off the branch.
10 The bear saved Gerard's life, for he landed safely on her body.

Page 73   Agreement of subject and verb

A
1 has
2 have
3 wasn't
4 weren't
5 try
6 tries

B
1 has
2 have
3 was
4 were
5 makes
6 make
7 are
8 is
9 give
10 gives

Page 74   Similes

A
1 rain
2 grave
3 Punch
4 eel
5 a lark
6 smooth
7 meek
8 mad
9 patient
10 proud

B   Revision
1 cucumber
2 fiddle
3 bee
4 doorpost
5 lion
6 bold
7 clean
8 dead
9 bright
10 sweet

C
1 Job
2 velvet
3 grave
4 doorpost
5 rain
6 lark
7 Punch
8 lamb

Page 75   Words which save work

A
1 recently
2 surrendered
3 postponed
4 talkative
5 speechless
6 occasionally
7 drought
8 survivors

B
1 accidentally
2 immediately
3 author
4 fearlessly
5 librarian
6 apologized
7 revolved

Page 76   Homophones

A
1 soar
5 berth
9 lessen

2 feint
6 guilt
10 route

3 bail
7 horde

4 site
8 stake

Page 77   Noises of creatures

A
1 trumpeting
2 barking
3 squealing
4 croaking
5 bleating
6 screeching, talking
7 chattering
8 gobbling

B
1 neigh
2 low
3 growl
4 apes
5 bulls
6 monkeys
7 hyenas
8 bay
9 sparrows
10 turkeys

C
1 bleating
2 baying
3 bellowed
4 chirping
5 screeching; talking
6 trumpeted
7 croaked

Page 78 Katy's narrow escape

1   She stuck the needle into Katy's chin.
2   She rushed to the gate where Clover stood waiting.
3   She was afraid of being late for school.
4   Katy was very cross.
5   She hurried into the playground and climbed onto the roof of the wood-shed.
6   The bonnet landed in the playground of Miller's School next door.
7   They would dance around it, pin it on a pole, use it as a football and wave it over the fence.
9   The friends stood rooted to the spot, astonished that Katy had returned safely from the Miller playground.

Page 79   Sounds

A

1 bow	2 bugle	3 bell
4 coins	5 feet	6 silk
7 brakes	8 brook	9 whip
10 bagpipes	11 swish	12 rattle; clatter
13 pop	14 ping	15 clatter
16 patter	17 report	18 jangle; rattle
19 clang	20 clap; peal	

B

1 whirr	2 peal	3 blast
4 clang	5 creak	6 wail
7 skirl	8 throb	

Page 80   Analogies

A	B	C
1 sty	1 pilot	1 headmaster; headmistress; head teacher
2 prince	2 sword	2 sole
3 rind	3 baker	3 patient
4 see; sight	4 wolf	4 water
5 port	5 deer	5 reptile
6 navy	6 drought	6 countess
7 hospital	7 elephant	7 deck

Page 81 Doers of actions

A
1. challenger
2. contributor
3. editor
4. president
5. liar
6. critic
7. applicant
8. operator
9. competitor
10. survivor

B
1. burglar
2. guardian
3. auctioneer
4. mutineer
5. captor
6. representative
7. dictator
8. opponent
9. successor
10. correspondent

Page 82 Twin words

A
1. fortune
4. neck
7. soul
10. spick

2. rough
5. call
8. rack
11. baggage

3. hearty
6. sixes
9. water
12. hue

B
1. ready
4. beck
7. fire
10. fame

2. neck
5. hue
8. ruin

3. body
6. bag
9. span

Page 83 Rhymes

A
1. bigger
4. red
7. skin
0. kin

2. figure
5. thin
8. chin
11. admire

3. head
6. pin
9. in
12. attire

B
1. work
   jerk
   shirk

2. home
   foam
   comb

3. grows
   chose
   froze

4. course
   force
   hoarse

5. become
   crumb
   glum

6. stole
   shoal
   scroll

7. nurse
   verse
   worse

8. cheer
   smear
   sphere

9. bought
   caught
   taught; taut

C
I have a garden of my own
Shining with flowers of every hue;
I loved it dearly while alone,
But I shall love it more with you;
And there the golden bees shall come
In summer-time at break of morn,
And wake us with their busy hum,
Around the Silea's fragrant thorn.

Page 84   A fight in a signal-tower

1   Marcus and Esca were by the parapet.
2   They dismounted in the courtyard below.
3   so far
4   Marcus thought that the tribesmen might be more useful to them alive than dead.
5   He kept it in his belt.
6   They were searching in the storehouse and guardroom.
7   Marcus described the tribesmen as fools because, by their shout, they had let Marcus and Esca know that they were coming up the stairway.
8   He had practised with the cestus.
9   The third tribesman, having seen his companions knocked down, had had some warning of what lay ahead of him.
10 He was unconscious.

Page 85   Double negatives

A

1   anything; nothing
2   anywhere; nowhere
3   anything; nothing
4   ever; never
5   anything; nothing
6   any; no

7   anybody; nobody
8   any; no
9   any; none
10 anyone; no one
11 anything; nothing
12 any; no

Page 86   Proverbs

A

1   a silver lining
2   at home
3   bite
4   A bird in the hand

B

1 is a friend indeed
2 iron is hot
3 at home
4 is sauce for the gander
5 is worth two in the bush
6 has a silver lining
7 to mend
8 saves nine
9 gathers no moss
10 mother of invention
11 leap

Give the meanings of Nos. 2, 3, 5, 8 and 9.

2 Carry out your plans when conditions are favourable.
3 Be kind to relatives before showing kindness to strangers.
5 It is wiser to accept an offer now than to depend on a better offer you may have in the future.
8 Repairs to any damage now will save bigger repairs later.
9 A person who flits from one job to another will never save money.

Page 87   Similes

A
1 death
2 dust
3 bat
4 thieves
5 lamb
6 sound
7 tender
8 timid
9 tough
10 large

B
1 lamb
2 Punch
3 Job
4 eel
5 velvet
6 clean
7 bright
8 bold
9 sweet
10 fit

C
1 death
2 mouse
3 leather
4 lamb
5 thieves
6 bat
7 life
8 bell
9 dust
10 bright

Page 88   Fun with words

A
1 stone
2 sacred
3 stare
4 seated
5 steed
6 drone
7 secret

B
1 create
2 carton
3 crêpe
4 carrot
5 treat
6 repair

C
1 bread; beard
2 spine; pines
3 dairy; diary
4 cried; cider

Page 89   Idioms

1   through the nose
2   feathering one's nest
3   to play second fiddle
4   to smell a rat
5   blowing his own trumpet

6   at loggerheads
7   a mountain out of a molehill
8   sent him to Coventry
9   French leave
10   the cold shoulder

Page 90   Long John Silver

1   The nickname was Barbecue.
2   He carried it by a lanyard round his neck.
3   It enabled him to have both hands as free as possible.
4   He wedged the foot of the crutch against a bulkhead to steady himself.
5   He had a line or two rigged up to help him across the widest spaces.
6   The coxswain told of the time when John, unarmed, had gripped four men and knocked their heads together.
7   The crew respected John for his learning, bravery and strength.
8   The parrot's name was Captain Flint.
9   He was named after a famous buccaneer.
10   He would throw his handkerchief over the cage.